THE GIRL ON THE VOLKSWAGEN FLOOR

"For true crime aficionados, a find! One of the most interesting books in the field in a long time."
—Los Angeles Times

"A potent narrative . . . Makes it clear that while truth may not really be stranger than fiction, it can certainly be even more engrossing, bewildering, and frustrating."
—Stanley Ellin, Noted Mystery Writer

"This is a fact-crime . . . which really reads like a novel . . . Quite amazing all the way."
—San Francisco Examiner & Chronicle

"This is a book that can, and should, be read in one sitting . . . Absolutely necessary to pause every so often just to let the tension drain off . . . A gripper of a nonfiction mystery . . . Terrific suspense which keeps the reader turning pages at a terrific pace just to find out what happened next . . . Compelling and frightening."
—The Houston [Texas] Post

"AS GRIPPING AND BIZARRE
AS THE MOST INVENTIVE WHODUNIT!"
—Saturday Review

The
Girl on the
Volkswagen
Floor

BY WILLIAM A. CLARK

A NATIONAL GENERAL COMPANY

This low-priced Bantam Book
has been completely reset in a type face
designed for easy reading, and was printed
from new plates. It contains the complete
text of the original hard-cover edition.
NOT ONE WORD HAS BEEN OMITTED.

THE GIRL ON THE VOLKSWAGEN FLOOR
A Bantam Book / published by arrangement with
Harper & Row, Publishers

PRINTING HISTORY
Harper & Row edition published July 1971
2nd printing . . . . *July 1971*
Bantam edition published June 1972

Bantam Books are published by Bantam Books, Inc., a National
General company. Its trade-mark, consisting of the words "Bantam
Books" and the portrayal of a bantam, is registered in the United
States Patent Office and in other countries. Marca Registrada.
Bantam Books, Inc., 666 Fifth Avenue, New York, N.Y. 10019.

PRINTED IN THE UNITED STATES OF AMERICA

For CHARLOTTE, my wife,
and in memory of
BARBARA and REGINA

Any man's death diminishes me,
because I am involved in mankind . . .

—*John Donne* (1573–1631)
DEVOTIONS

1

In June of 1968 I was a newspaper reporter in Dayton, Ohio. I had had fourteen years' experience as a reporter. I had been a sportswriter at a World Series . . . a six-foot-five-inch, 210-pound "sob sister" at VIP funerals . . . a gatherer of facts and opinions at disasters. I had seen bodies fished out of the Ohio River after the Silver Bridge went down and I had seen parts of bodies dug from the rubble of Richmond, Indiana, after a downtown business block blew up. I had been a police reporter who had covered many murders without becoming involved in any (most crime stories bored me and I had a strong preference for humor over homicide). I had seen the United States from coast to coast and England from seaside to Midlands. I had been in Canada one week and in Mexico the next. I had lived the loose, carefree life of a bachelor until I was thirty-four, and thought I had a broad knowledge of the world. I had no belief in psychic phenomena or extrasensory perception.

Then, when I was thirty-six, married, and the father of a six-month-old daughter, on Thursday, June 13, 1968, the nude body of a young woman was discovered in a Dayton suburb. The initial indication was that the victim had been raped and murdered. If the body had been found in the 272,000-population central city of Dayton, I might have said, "So what? It's just another murder and we had fifty-eight of them in Dayton in 1967—an average of better than one per week." However, the body had not been found in Dayton; it had been found in a middle-class suburb of 72,000 where there had never before been a sex murder and where there was a widely held belief that such a thing "can't happen here." I asked questions. From the answers I got I became convinced that the crime was more than unusual—it was bizarre and bordered on the fantastic.

I was fascinated—almost hypnotized—by a mystery that grew—riddle by puzzle, mistake by misunderstanding, jealousy by suspicion—into a vast maze of unanswered questions and improbable occurrences for which there seemed to have been no logical entrance and to be no possible exit.

My search for answers to the mystery was long and sometimes maddening. I touched some nerves along the way and heard cleverly veiled threats made against my wife and myself. I changed from a carefree man, who never bothered to lock his doors or windows at night, into a confused person who slept with a loaded pistol beside his bed.

But, in the end, I knew.

2

It all began on Wednesday, June 12, 1968—a day when even the weather was a bit of a mystery in southwestern Ohio. A tornado watch had been in effect during the night as an intense heat wave passed out of the area. The morning was sunny, cool, and pleasant. In the afternoon temperatures were in the high seventies and skies were overcast in the Greater Dayton area.

The Dayton metropolitan area is a composite of separate political subdivisions each with its own law-enforcement agency—the result of the post-World War II population explosion out of the central cities which caused existing suburbs to mushroom in size and new suburbs to be formed and incorporated alongside the old. The city of Dayton remained the commercial and industrial heart of the area; but much of the money and the brains were in the suburbs. The city of Kettering was the largest (1968 estimated population 72,000) and most heavily middle-class of the twenty-one suburban townships, villages, and cities ringing the city of Dayton. The spirit of separatism ran deep among the many law-enforcement agencies. (Twenty-nine different emergency police numbers are listed on the inside front cover of the Dayton telephone directory; the numbers are those of twenty-five police departments, three county sheriff's departments, and the Ohio State Highway Patrol.) When a major crimes squad (to be manned by the area's most experienced police personnel) was proposed, a Dayton detective said,

"It'll never work because of all the jealousy between departments. We need a metropolitan police force. It'll have to come to that someday. These hoods don't wait to see whose jurisdiction they're in before they act. They don't worry about county or city lines. But we have to!"

Early in the afternoon of Wednesday, June 12, Miss Barbara Ann Butler, wearing a blue-and-white bikini, went to the pool at her suburban Dayton apartment complex. "She was there with two nurses who live in the apartment next door to her," according to the pool director, Mrs. Linda Dietz. Mrs. Dietz knew Barbara Butler as a "nice, attractive young teacher" and a sunbather. She said, "Barbara always sunbathed in exactly the same spot at the pool . . . but never went in the water."

In downtown Dayton, a newspaper photographer noted black clouds swirling overhead and told a reporter, "I want to get these outside shots taken first. It's gonna rain like hell any minute now—and when it does—I want me and my equipment to be inside someplace."

The approaching storm put an end to Barbara Butler's sunbathing. She decided to leave the pool area at the Woodman Park Drive Apartments, a complex of modern middle-income units located just outside of Dayton's eastern city limits in the Montgomery County political subdivision of Mad River Township. "I'm going to Kettering to do some shopping," she informed her two poolside companions. "I hear they have great bargains at the Ontario Store down there. Any of you guys want to come along?"

The two friends declined Barbara's invitation to accompany her to the Ontario Discount Store in Kettering. The friends were enjoying a Wednesday afternoon off from their jobs as Kettering doctors' office nurses. They remained at the pool while Barbara returned to her apartment to change into street clothes. Miss Butler had resided in the Dayton area for only ten months prior to June 12, 1968. This was to be her first trip to the Ontario Store.

About 2:00 P.M., a neighbor saw Barbara Butler leave her townhouse apartment and walk toward a parking lot. "What stuck in my mind," the neighbor recalled, "was that she was wearing a pant-dress and a cute white triangle scarf." Barbara got in her car and drove off.

A few minutes later, Barbara parked her 1967 silver-blue Volkswagen in front of the apartment-complex rental office. She got out of the car, entered the office, and was inside "two or three minutes at the most," an office employee said. Barbara's purpose for stopping at the rental office was to apply for a pool pass. She said she wanted the pass for a male guest she was expecting for the weekend. The request was denied because the friend was not going to be a "bona fide guest" staying overnight in Barbara's apartment. Then, the office employee recalled, "Miss Butler just smiled, turned, and walked out the door."

It takes between fifteen and twenty minutes, depending on traffic volume and traffic-light luck, to drive from the Woodman Park Drive Apartments' rental office to the Ontario Discount Store. Distance and direction from the apartment complex to the store is approximately five miles southwest —the distance varies by a few tenths of a mile depending upon which of two routes a person chooses halfway in the journey between apartment complex and store.

The store is located in a built-up area of suburban-mix architecture (drive-in restaurant, apartment house, self-service car wash, school, store) in the city of Kettering.

Kettering is an 18.01-square-mile sprawl of residences and shopping centers located south of Dayton on the eastern edge of Montgomery County. Its boundaries are city-limits signs which stand, almost as if by chance, in the midst of residential blocks on boulevard-type thoroughfares over which the majority of Kettering's inhabitants commute daily to their sources of income in Dayton. Many Kettering residents think of their address as a status symbol and compare their suburb with the central city in these terms: "Kettering is a place to live, Dayton is just a place to work."

Kettering, named for inventor Charles F. Kettering, was the result of the postwar "flight to the suburbs" of Dayton's middle class. It was, according to its official motto, "founded on progress" as a village in 1952. City status was reached in 1955. In the next ten years Kettering's population increased 47 percent, making it, according to town boosters, "the fastest growing city in Ohio."

In 1968 Kettering was an all-white "bedroom" community where there were no slums and no heavy industries. The town's assets, according to a chamber of commerce fact sheet, included: "Mostly single family houses, owner occupied, half over $20,000 in valuation . . . real estate tax: $41.80 per $1,000 assessed at 41 percent of the market value (annual tax on a $25,000 home amounts to $428.45) . . . rental housing scarce . . . apartments of various types

4

readily available . . . $12,808 average income per household . . . 65 percent of high school graduates enter college . . . 19.39 high school pupil-teacher ratio . . . Protestant and Catholic churches . . . city manager–council government . . . (numerous) civic organizations . . . 107 acres of parks and 20 miles of bikeways."

Barbara Ann Butler must have arrived at the Ontario Discount Store, 2800 Wilmington Pike, Kettering, about 2:30 P.M. on June 12. The sky was still dark and threatening, but there had been no precipitation as yet. If Miss Butler had any fears other than one of getting rained upon, she did not express them. The store, which boasts "discounts for thrifty shoppers" on a wide variety of merchandise ranging from name-brand appliances to housebrand groceries, is a large, one-story structure set far back from one of Kettering's busiest streets at the eastern extremity of a paved, four-acre parking lot.

Shopping at Ontario should have been a pleasant experience for Barbara Butler that Wednesday afternoon: there were hundreds of free spaces for her little Volkswagen in the store's huge parking lot; an equal number of four-wheeled shopping carts were available at the store's main entrance; and there were very few other shoppers in the store, so she could stroll leisurely through aisles of items, listening to soft music piped in over a public-address system—with only an occasional interruption for the announcement of a "special" bargain—as she made her selections in air-conditioned comfort.

At a checkout counter Barbara Butler removed from her shopping cart: floor wax, floor wax remover, a mop, a ten-pound bag of charcoal, and a cardboard box containing a twenty-four-pound cast-iron hibachi barbecue. The checkout clerk inspected the items, processed their prices through her cash register, and asked for $13.72 in payment. Barbara Butler offered a check, drawn on a newly opened account, for the exact amount of purchase. The checkout clerk refused the check in accordance with a store policy that discouraged the cashing of checks, especially those drawn on unpersonalized, newly opened accounts. There was a discussion which developed into an issue of "Take my check or I'll have to take back the merchandise."

The store manager was summoned. Barbara explained that she thought it unsafe for a single girl to go unescorted in public with cash on her person. She showed the manager and the clerk that she had only a small amount of change in a wallet she carried in her brown straw purse. The manager said later that he approved Barbara's check for cashing because he was "sympathetic to her problem. My wife and I recently moved to the Dayton area from another state," he explained, "and my wife had trouble getting a check cashed."

The tornado threat had passed without incident; now, so too had the rain clouds. The parking lot outside the store was bathed in midafternoon sunshine.

The checkout clerk and the store manager watched Barbara Butler push her cart full of purchases toward an exit door. They recalled later that she stopped just before she went out the door to take a pair of sunglasses out of her purse and put them on. "I saw her go out the door," the clerk said. "But that's all I remember—I don't know whether she turned left, or right, or walked straight ahead into the parking lot."

Barbara Butler walked out the door of the Ontario store sometime between 3:30 and 3:45 P.M. on Wednesday, June 12. (The checkout clerk told police later that she received a long-distance telephone call "not too long after the girl left the store." Telephone company records indicated that the call was placed at 3:48 P.M. The clerk was unsure of how much time elapsed between Miss Butler's exit from the store and the telephone call; she could only estimate the time period as having been "less than twenty minutes, but maybe only three or four minutes.") The remaining hours of her life were shrouded in a fog of mystery of which a few wisps will always remain.

At 11:06 P.M. on Wednesday, June 12, a Miss Donna Gray (a pseudonym) telephoned the Mad River Township Police Department and requested that an officer be dispatched to 4957 Woodman Park Drive, apartment 9. Miss Gray insisted that the police "do something because my roommate went to the store this afternoon and never came home."

The high temperature in the Dayton area that day was 79 degrees at 3:30 P.M.—the earliest possible time of Barbara's disappearance. No rain fell but the temperature plummeted in late afternoon and early evening. At 8:05 P.M., Kettering's UHF Channel 16 began televising the 1931 film version of Theodore Dreiser's *An American Tragedy*. Sunset was at 9:06 P.M. The low temperature for the day was 55 degrees

6

at 11:55 P.M.—just as Mad River Township Patrolman John DeHaven was about to leave Barbara Butler's apartment to forward a description of her to all police agencies in the Greater Dayton area.

Miss Barbara Ann Butler—white, female, twenty-three; a five-foot-four-inch, 110-pound brunette believed to be driving a 1967 silver-blue Volkswagen—had now officially become a missing person. Her whereabouts was unknown, but it was assumed that she was somewhere in the Dayton metropolitan area of 1,715 square miles and 900,000 people. A loop teletype broadcast alerted all police agencies in the area to be "on the lookout" for Miss Butler. However, the actual missing-person *investigation* into her whereabouts was the concern of only the police with jurisdiction in the area which Miss Butler had been reported missing from: the Mad River Township section of Montgomery County. Two agencies had police powers in this area: the tiny Mad River Township Police Department of one full-time chief and two part-time patrolmen and the much larger Montgomery County Sheriff's Department. A Mad River patrolman took the missing-person complaint, but Sheriff's Detective Les King was assigned to investigate it.

Mr. and Mrs. Bernard Butler, the parents of the missing girl, went to the Montgomery County sheriff's headquarters in downtown Dayton on the morning of Thursday, June 13, to talk with Detective King. The parents told the detective that they had driven to Dayton that morning from their home in Westerville (a suburb of Columbus, Ohio, located eighty miles northeast of Dayton) after their daughter's roommate had phoned to inform them that Barbara had been missing overnight. King said later that he could tell from information provided by the parents that "it wasn't like Barbara to just go off somewhere."

Thursday, June 13, was a sunny but unusually cool mid-June day for southwestern Ohio. About 5:00 P.M., Miss Loretta Carmody (a pseudonym) entered the Ontario Discount Store and asked for assistance. She identified herself as a nurse whose "neighbor friend is missing." She insisted that "I need someone to come out to the parking lot with me, because my friend's car is in your lot and we better look and see what's inside it."

A store employee went out to the parking lot with Miss Carmody. They checked the doors of a silver-blue 1967

7

Volkswagen and found them locked. They looked through the windows of the car and saw:

—On the right front passenger-side floor: a pair of sunglasses and a yellow towel on top of a white blanket with pink-and-green floral designs.

—On the driver's-side floor: a large brown wicker-type woman's straw handbag.

—On the front seat: nothing.

—On the back seat: a filled grocery bag with a blue washcloth atop it, a cardboard box, and a bag of charcoal.

At the urging of Miss Carmody, the store employee, a teen-age youth, forced open the right cozy wing and reached an arm inside the Volkswagen so that he could touch the blanket. The boy felt more than a blanket on the floor of the little Volkswagen; and when his mind realized that his fingers were poking at the features of a human being: "The boy," a witness said, "really let out a whoop!"

It was 5:10 P.M. The parking lot was crowded with shoppers. Attracted by the youth's scream, people ran to the Volkswagen and looked inside it. The boy pointed to the blanket on the front floor of the car and claimed that there was a body beneath it. People scoffed. One man said, "I'll have to see it to believe it."

A female store security officer arrived. She reached in through the open vent window, unlocked the door, and opened it.

The blanket was pulled back.

There was a body.

There was pandemonium.

Many people got into the car, contaminating true evidence and putting down false evidence. Eventually someone thought to notify the Kettering police. The death scene was then restored to a facsimile of its original appearance.

Police roared onto the lot, got out of their cruisers, went to the Volkswagen, and looked inside it. They saw a pair of sunglasses on top of a towel atop a blanket on the floor and asked, "Where's the body?" To answer their own question police reopened the car, pulled back the blanket and saw what one officer thought "must be the body of a child because there ain't enough room in a Volkswagen for it to be an adult."

Loretta Carmody corrected the officer. She identified the

8

body as being that of her twenty-three-year-old friend and neighbor. Barbara Ann Butler's body had been found in the very same store parking lot that she had disappeared into twenty-five and a half hours earlier.

Police assumed that the victim had been raped and murdered. Next, they had to determine where these alleged crimes took place in order to establish venue. (Literally, *venue* means the place in which alleged events from which a legal action arises take place; more to the point, however, venue was the answer to a very important question facing the Kettering police: which police agency among the many in the Greater Dayton area was going to have to do the work of investigating the alleged homicide of Barbara Ann Butler?) There was no evidence in or about the Volkswagen that would establish—as a definite fact—that the victim had met her fate in the parking lot or any other place within the venue of the Kettering Police Department. Witnesses to the alleged crime also were lacking. The body had been found in a car—as mobile an alleged crime scene as ever there was (the Volkswagen might have been anywhere when, and if, the murder occurred inside it).

The question of venue in the alleged homicide was further complicated by the fact that the victim had been the subject of a missing-person investigation. The Kettering police did not have venue in the missing-person case. The discovery of Miss Butler's body established her whereabouts as the Ontario Discount Store parking lot in the city of Kettering and solved the missing-person case in Mad River Township and Montgomery County. At this point all investigative procedures were technically at a standstill and venue in the suspected crime of homicide was open to debate.

A high-ranking Montgomery County law-enforcement officer later told me this version of how the matter of venue was informally, but effectively, resolved:

A Montgomery County sheriff's detective assigned to the missing-person investigation arrived on the Ontario Store lot. A Kettering detective greeted the sheriff's detective and then said:

"The girl must have been murdered out in the county somewhere and her body brought back here and dumped. It looks like a real sticky sex crime for you guys, but I want you to know that we'll cooperate and try to help you solve it in any way that we can."

9

The county detective stepped back, pointed to the Volkswagen, and roared out these points:

"There's the car!

"There's the body!

"We're in Kettering!

"You ain't stickin' me with no damn homicide!"

Venue in the alleged crime of homicide was thus established as being the city of Kettering—unless and until such a time as the Kettering police could prove that the scene of the crime was a place outside their venue.

A homicide isn't officially a homicide until a county coroner rules it so after a postmortem examination of the body. When violence is suspected upon the discovery of a body in Kettering, Ohio, the proper procedure is: stand back, notify the office of the Montgomery County coroner, secure the area of the death scene, and await the arrival of the coroner's representative.

The Montgomery County coroner's office was notified "about an hour" after the discovery of Miss Butler's body. Coroner's Investigator Gene Roberts arrived on the Ontario Store lot about 7:00 P.M. He took color photographs of the death scene. Then he took notes which, freely translated, said:

The body is lying on its right side . . . hands up against the chest with fists clenched . . . nails long and unbroken . . . head jammed tightly against the passenger side door . . . the victim's hair is dark brown and trimmed medium short, fitting the head . . . there is a bruise under the right eye . . . a trail of postmortem blood extends from the nose to the lips, to the middle of the chest, and off to a large spot of dried blood on the right breast . . . a dot of blood is visible on the left breast . . . there are marks on the neck which are discontinuous over the nape and throat . . . the left forearm is bound with adhesive tape . . . a loop of tape dangles from the left arm . . . the right forearm bears adhesive marks indicating that the right arm was pulled free of the tape . . . a pair of white nylon panties are draped over the right forearm . . . dried blood excretions are present in the genital area and a used tampon is beside the body . . . the right leg is shoved under the instrument panel and bent back at the knee immediately above the brake and accelerator pedals of the auto . . . the left leg extends outward until it is bent back at the knee and jammed up against the floor manual shift lever . . . one brown sandal is upon the left foot, another sandal is beside the body.

While the coroner's investigator was making his preliminary body examination, Kettering detectives took measurements and searched the car for evidence. Stuffed under the victim's legs they found:

A yellow, sleeveless, zipper-back pant-dress decorated with brown, green, and red floral designs; a white scarf and a yellow brassiere. There was a double rip in the neckband of the dress which became a single rip extending down the front to the crotch area, across to the center of the left pant leg and then down it through the hem; a similar rip extended upward from the hem of the right pant leg and then across to within an inch of the main rip coming down from the neck; the neckline zipper on the back of the dress was closed. The clip to the left bra strap was undone, but there were torn threads on the right bra strap, indicating that it had been forcibly removed from the body. There was a blood spot in the left cup of the bra.

The ashtrays of the car were filled with butts and several neat piles of ashes were found on the driver's-side floor near the handbag. A wallet containing a small amount of change and the personal papers of the victim—driver's license, receipts, credit cards, and social security card—was found in the handbag along with a glass case and a key chain with several keys attached. None of the keys fitted the ignition or door locks of the Volkswagen—the car key was missing.

The car was dusted for prints. Numerous finger and palm prints were lifted. A complete vacuum cleaning of the car produced several shades and lengths of human hair, a brown string, and a quantity of fiber tatters that appeared to be from the victim's pant-dress.

The items in the packages on the back seat were checked against a sales slip. None of the items purchased by Miss Butler in the store the day before were missing, but something new had been added—inside the grocery bag with the floor wax, the floor wax remover, and the unassembled mop was a small piece of blue terry cloth. The edges of the cloth were tattered, indicating that it had been ripped out of a larger piece of similar material—not the blue washcloth which had been found on top of the grocery bag; it, as well as the yellow towel atop the blanket, was intact.

The standard "beetle" type Volkswagen was, itself, the best part of a ton of potential evidence. In addition to fingerprints, the 1,676-pound vehicle had rust spots and paint chips over the front trunk hood and a considerable amount of a black substance, which appeared to be paving tar, on the wheels, undercarriage, and fenders.

At approximately 7:30 P.M. the coroner's investigator ordered the body removed to the morgue for autopsy. He impounded the car and directed that it be towed to a garage for storage. The body was picked up and lifted from the car. There—on the floor mat where the body had been—was a single key to the car.

At 11:30 P.M. on Thursday, June 13, Montgomery County Coroner Dr. Robert Zipf began a postmortem examination of the body. The autopsy was completed at 1:30 A.M. on June 14. The findings were:

The death was a homicide.

The body had *not* been sexually molested in any way—the victim was, in fact, a virgin.

The cause of death was asphyxiation due to strangulation. A ligature—either the scarf or some other narrow, cordlike device—had been used to cause the strangulation. The cause of death was not associated with alcohol or carbon monoxide. The blood alcohol level was negative. Carbon monoxide was present in only a minimal amount—less than 5 percent.

Body injuries were marks made by the ligature on the sides of the neck, a small mark on the left ear similar to the marks on the neck, a bruise under the right eye, other bruises over the top of the head, and a dot of blood on the left breast. In length and appearance, the strangulation marks were longer and more pronounced on the left side of the neck. In width, the marks varied from six-tenths of an inch down to two-tenths of an inch. The marks were discontinuous over the throat and the nape of the neck. The bruises were due to blows sufficient to cause momentary unconsciousness, but not death. The dot of blood may have been caused by the holding of a knife point against the left breast, or it may have been due to a burst pimple.

Time of death was about 11:00 P.M. on Wednesday, June 12.

The stomach contained two thimblefuls of a brown substance—possibly the remnants of a light snack or soft drink consumed as either a late breakfast or an early lunch.

The bladder was empty.

The body, except for dried excretions of vaginal blood in the genital area, was exceptionally clean. (There were no traces of urine on the body. Also, there were no stains of urine or vaginal blood on the victim's clothing or in her car. Coroner's Chief Investigator Harry Bloomer said that urination occurs in 90 percent of all deaths by asphyxiation whenever the bladder is half full or more at death.) There were no obvious indications of a major struggle: the fingernails were not torn and there was no foreign matter beneath the nails.

The blood above the ligature marks—usually quite black in a strangulation death—was unusually red.

3

On Friday, June 14, the Barbara Butler murder case was the top news story in the Dayton area. Teams of newspaper, television, and radio reporters scrambled for details. Kettering police received newsmen courteously, but declined to answer questions related to details of the investigation on the grounds that this was confidential information. Kettering Police Chief John R. Shryock did, however, confirm the existence of a mystery. He told reporters that "There are at present no suspects in the case."

I knew that the Kettering police would have to come up with a suspect within a matter of hours or else the mystery would grow deeper with each tick of the clock. There is a detective's maxim that a murder case will be solved if suspicion centers on one suspect, or one group of suspects, within the first twenty-four hours of the investigation; however, if there is no prime suspect after twenty-four hours, the odds that the case will go unsolved will increase with each additional hour that passes.

I also was aware that the known facts of a mystery are aids to the solution of it only if the facts fit together to form some indication of the total picture of the mystery. But the known facts of the Butler case were a paradox: they raised more questions than they answered. Actually, the facts seldom jibed with one another even when assumptions were made in an attempt figuratively to glue them together.

This is the picture—and some of the puzzles—that appeared in my mind from my knowledge of the facts:

A girl had gone to a suburban store on a Wednesday afternoon. She was seen leaving the store about 3:45 P.M. She had not returned to her apartment by 11 P.M., so her roommate reported her missing. The next afternoon the missing girl's body was found in her car in the store parking lot as the result of a search instituted by a neighbor. The coroner ruled that the girl had been murdered about 11:00 P.M. on Wednesday.

These facts raised the following questions: Was it just a coincidence that the girl was reported missing at approximately the same time that she died? Why did the neighbor ask a store employee to open the car? If she was so anxious to know what was under the blanket, why didn't she force open the cozy wing and reach her own hand inside the car?

According to the Kettering police: the times were apparently just a coincidence and the neighbor did not know exactly why she took the course of action that she did take— she just thought that "it was the proper thing to do."

I then wondered if it was possible for the girl to have been murdered without ever having left the parking lot. I found out that the parking lot was frequented by shoppers until after the store closed at 10:00 P.M.; that the lot was in natural light until about 9:30 P.M. and that it was well lit by floodlights after that time. So I had to agree with a Kettering detective who said, "We can't visualize the whole thing having taken place in that lot."

If not the lot, where? Police appealed to the public for information and made extensive checks in an attempt to establish the girl's whereabouts in the seven-hour gap between the time she was known to have left the store on Wednesday afternoon and the time that the coroner said she died on Wednesday evening. Police reported that they could find no one who would admit to having seen the girl between 3:45 P.M. and 11:00 P.M. on June 12. Police said their investigation had produced no information that would indicate that Miss Butler might have returned to her apartment from the store. If this was so, then the easiest way to explain the girl's fate was to assume that her body had been returned to the parking lot after she had been abducted from the lot, taken to a remote place, and murdered. But, as a detective said, "This implies a quick death—about five o'clock or so. The eleven-o'clock time of death set by the coroner is too late—it doesn't fit with the abduction theory when other facts of the autopsy are considered."

The empty bladder and the urine-stain-free body . . . the menstrual cycle and a clean pair of white panties . . . the absence of any indications that the girl had struggled with her killer: all these factors made it seem unlikely that the virgin girl had been forcibly taken from the parking lot and held prisoner in a remote place for seven hours by a person she feared might take her honor, if not her life, at any moment. I presented the abduction theory and the autopsy facts to several women as a hypothetical situation and asked them what they would do under similar circumstances. All the answers were along these lines: "I would have tried to scratch his eyes out, kick, done anything. If that didn't work, I would have been so scared that I would have urinated and spotted my pants."

On the other hand, the coroner found that the victim's stomach was empty. He said that the girl had eaten only a light snack on the day of her disappearance. She must have been hungry. Why, then, if she had not been held under duress, hadn't she eaten an evening meal? Because she died before her suppertime?

I wondered if the time of death might have been in error by several hours. I asked Montgomery County Coroner Zipf this question: "Is it possible that the girl might have died many hours before eleven o'clock? About five o'clock, perhaps?"

Dr. Zipf answered, "The girl died about eleven o'clock according to our best medical knowledge. There is no mystic manner for determining time of death—you just go by the facts of rigidity and body temperature. Rigor mortis comes on at a certain time and disappears at a certain time; also we take the body temperature of a corpse—knowing that the temperature will have dropped a certain number of degrees each hour since death—and count back to normal."

I asked, "How much leeway is there in the term 'about eleven o'clock'?"

Coroner's Chief Investigator Bloomer answered, "Three hours either way. The exact time of death could have been any time between eight o'clock in the evening of Wednesday, June 12, and two o'clock in the morning of Thursday, June

15

13. The six-hour spread centered on eleven o'clock is necessary because of several unknowns. The unknowns are: the length of time the nude body was lying upon the floor mat of the car; the length of time the body was covered by the blanket; the length of time the car was parked out of doors on a cool evening—the car and body could have been in a heated garage for part of the time; and the exact temperature of the victim at time of death."

I came away from the coroner's office thinking: Good God! Now we're talking about a time of death that might have been as much as ten and one-half hours after the girl was last seen alive walking into the store parking lot. And the earliest possible time of death—eight o'clock—doesn't fit with the abduction theory any better than eleven o'clock does. It's still too late . . . too much time to account for . . . three too many hours, at least."

The time of death—one of the few "definite facts" of the mystery—was thus a hindrance, rather than a help, to an unraveling of the mystery.

The most startling autopsy finding, however, was that the victim had not been sexually molested. This fact (it could almost be labeled an "unfact") made it difficult for the police to categorize the murder as a sex crime. The nature of the crime, the motive, and the sex of the killer could only be assumed. Police do not like to work from assumptions; they want, as the old joke says, "the facts, ma'am, just the facts." However, the Kettering police had to start somewhere: they assumed that Barbara Butler's murder was "a sex crime, probably." This established a motive, and the killer's sex. Or did it? What kind of male sexual deviate would murder an attractive girl without raping her?

The cause of death and the marks on the neck conjured up a mystery of their own. The coroner said that the girl had been strangled with some type of narrow cord which had left marks on the sides of the neck. There were no strangulation marks on either the front or the back of the neck. There was a mark on the left ear that was similar to the marks on the sides of the neck. It was speculated that the mark on the ear had been made as the result of the killer forcibly slipping the nose of the cord around the neck of the victim. But what a rub this was! If a cord had been tied all the way around the neck—why didn't the marks left by the cord go all the way around the neck? The coroner had no certain explanation as to how a healthy adult could have been strangled into a state of asphyxia and death by pressure from a cord that apparently had not been tied about the circumference of the neck. He could only speculate that if asphyxiation had resulted from a cord being held against the sides of the neck—death would have been extremely slow and painful. This, in turn, again led to a sense of wonder about the absence of any obvious indications of a major struggle. Wouldn't any conscious human being attempt to struggle with an assailant in the course of a slow and painful death? Miss Butler's forearms had been taped together, but this would not entirely immobilize her hands and nails. She had suffered a black eye and other blows on top of her head; but the coroner said that these injuries would cause only momentary unconsciousness. The victim had not been drunk or overcome by carbon monoxide. She might have been drugged. However, the coroner said this possible answer for the absence of a struggle could not be determined until the completion of tissue and acid-extraction studies. The results of the drug tests, police were informed, would not be available for some time.

Coroner Zipf typed the murder as being "not a crime of vengeance or passion in the classic sense. There was nothing in her injuries that indicates severe punishment. It was daintily done . . . probably, lividity indicates, while the victim was seated on the right front seat of the Volkswagen."

The evidence in the car and on the body answered one question and posed a score of others:

All of the victim's purchases and possessions were in the car—so robbery was ruled out as a motivation factor. Instead of something being taken, something had apparently been added: the swatch of blue terry cloth found in the shopping bag. Miss Butler's close friends said that they had never seen the victim display the swatch of cloth or heard her mention it. Was it, then, something that the killer had left behind? Was it the remnant of a rag that the killer had used to mop up his fingerprints?

The victim's forearms had been taped together—and then the right arm had been pulled free of the tape. Had the killer freed the right arm to make it easier for him to rip the pant-dress from the body? Why had he ripped the dress off? To make it appear that she had been sexually molested?

A single car key was found on the floor of the car. Miss Butler's friends said that she had two car keys and kept them on the key chain found in the handbag. Had the killer taken the keys off the key chain and thrown one of them down on the floor? Why would he touch either of the car keys—at some risk of leaving a fingerprint on them—unless he needed to touch a car key? What purpose might a key to a 1967 model Volkswagen serve the killer? It was both a door and an ignition key. The 1967 model Volkswagen could be locked from the outside without a key, so the killer had not needed the key to lock the car doors. There was only one logical reason why the killer needed the key—to drive the car. Drive the car where? From the parking lot to another place and then back to the lot? Was the victim abducted from the lot in her own car and taken to a more secluded place to be murdered? If so, why drive the car back to the lot? Why not leave the car and body in the secluded place where the chances of immediate discovery were less likely than in a busy parking lot? Had the killer wanted the crime to be quickly known? Or was there some more likely reason why the killer returned the car and body to the lot? Because his own car was parked on the lot, perhaps? But it was not at all certain that killer and victim had met in the parking lot. Maybe Miss Butler had left the parking lot willingly and alone. If so, she had met her killer in a place other than the parking lot. What other place? Why, then, would the killer drive the car and body back to the parking lot? Because the murder scene was the killer's place of residence? Other tacks could be taken and other possibilities raised. And, having found one key, the police had to ask themselves: Where is the second key?

The bizarre manner in which Miss Butler's body was left by her killer—under a blanket topped by a yellow towel* and a pair of sunglasses—posed this question: Was the purpose of the covering items one of concealment? or veneration? or attraction?

In theory, arguments could be made for all three purposes. They went like this:

One—The blanket was placed over the body by the killer for the sole purpose of concealing it from view while driving back to the parking lot from the murder scene. Then the

---

* Police said that their investigation determined that these items "were logically in the car and were seen in the car before the day of the murder." The blanket was Miss Butler's property. The yellow towel found on top of the body and the blue washcloth found in the back seat were the property of a girlfriend, who was a student nurse and part-time laboratory technician at the county morgue.

towel and sunglasses were "just tossed" atop the blanket as the last acts of a killer bent on making certain that all of Miss Butler's effects were left in the car with the body.

Two—The items were placed over the body as a "tender loving care" gesture by a person who hated Miss Butler enough to kill her but loved her enough to venerate and protect her body. The sunglasses rested on top of the towel with both temples open. This indicated that the glasses were carefully and purposely placed there as the crown for some weird form of monument. One detective said, "The way that body was in the car with all that junk on top of it makes me wonder if the killer didn't think he had buried her and then put up his own gravestone."

Three—The handbag and other items on the front floor of the car and the packages on the back seat were meant as an attraction for a thief. The killer left valuable items lying about in hopes that a thief would break into the car, leave his fingerprints in the car and on the items in the car, lift the blanket, discover the body and flee in such a panic that he would be observed and suspected as the murderer.

All three arguments were logical. But, perhaps, all three of them were wrong because the killer may have had no logical reason for killing and no logical reason for abandoning the body the way he did. Thus the only certain indication provided by the careful packaging of the body and effects was that the killer had been able to do so in an unhurried manner without fear of observation.

A detective said, "There are so many screwy angles to this case, I could theorize on it from now until doomsday without getting any real answers." Too many parts of the puzzle were missing. Why? Was it simply due to blind luck? Or was it the result of an almost fiendish scheme plotted and carried out by a very clever individual?

4

On Saturday, June 15, I was working the Dayton *Daily News* police beat. I phoned Kettering police headquarters to inquire if there had been any overnight developments in the Butler case; I was told that police had "nothing new" to report.

I was depressed. I had only one obvious story to write: a "fear story" based on my knowledge that time was on the side of Barbara Butler's killer. Every minute that passed made it less and less likely that the person responsible for the crime would be apprehended and removed from society. I feared that if the murderer was not caught, then all females in the Dayton area—my wife and daughter included—were potential victims of a phantomlike individual who had apparently been able to kill without leaving behind any clue to his identity. I did not want to write a "fear story." I tried to think of another angle.

I picked up a copy of Friday's final edition and looked at the victim's picture. I saw an oval-faced, smiling, wide-eyed girl, with short, dark hair. I wondered: What kind of weirdo would kill a girl like this? A girl like what? All I knew about Barbara Butler was that she was an unmarried schoolteacher who shared a townhouse apartment with another schoolteacher named Donna Gray.

I walked up to the city desk and announced: "I'm gonna go talk to Donna Gray. She was the dead girl's roommate . . . maybe she can tell me some things about Butler that will give us an idea why somebody wanted to kill her."

"Lots of luck," a deskman snapped. "Didn't you hear?"

"Hear what?"

"That Donna Gray moved out of her apartment bag and baggage sometime yesterday and has gone God knows where. No forwarding address, no nothing—just gone!"

I went to Kettering police headquarters and asked the detective in charge of the Butler investigation, "Where is the roommate? Why did she skip town? Is she a suspect?"

Detective Sergeant Jim Tobias answered, "She is in the Columbus area. She did not skip town—she had previous plans to move out of the apartment on Thursday evening. I cannot class her as a suspect . . . she has cooperated with us fully."

I explained to the detective why I wanted to talk to Donna Gray. I asked for her address.

"Miss Gray has requested that her whereabouts not be divulged."

"Why?"

"For reasons of personal safety and to keep away crank calls and such."

"Do you believe that Miss Gray is in danger?"

"No, but I must honor her request that we keep her whereabouts confidential."

Tobias then claimed that Barbara Butler's disappearance and death had delayed, not encouraged, her roommate's departure from the Dayton area. "She had planned to move out on Thursday, but had to hold up a day because of what happened," he said. "Miss Butler and Miss Gray had both resigned their schoolteaching jobs this spring. Butler was going to stay on in the apartment, but Gray was moving to Columbus in order to attend summer school at Ohio State and then get married sometime in August."

I stared at the detective. Then I said, "Pardon me, but would you run that one by me again?"

Tobias repeated the statement and insisted that his investigation had determined the truth of it.

"Where does your investigation stand at the moment?"

"We still have no suspects," the detective answered, "but every man in the department is working on the case and we aren't paying any attention to the clock in our attempts to find a suspect. We are awaiting a laboratory report on possible fingerprints found in the car and on items in the car. We are still attempting to establish the victim's whereabouts in the time gap between her departure from the store and her death."

"What kind of girl was Barbara Butler?"

"We have learned from interviews with the dead girl's acquaintances that she was a normal-type person who had a normal number of dates. We have been talking to men who have had dates with her as far back as last Christmas. One of these men 'broke up' with the victim a week and a half before her death. Miss Butler was a good upstanding girl and not the type who would associate with strangers . . . she was definitely not the bar-going type."

I asked for the boyfriends' names and was told that the names were confidential information. I asked about the boyfriend that Barbara Butler had unsuccessfully sought a pool pass for on the day of her death. I was told that police had verified that he was 150 miles north of Dayton in the Toledo area on the day of Miss Butler's disappearance and death. "He is *not* a suspect," Tobias insisted.

I had spent an hour talking with the prime authority on the murder investigation and had learned that the victim was a nice girl who dated boys. I left the Kettering police station convinced that if I wanted more answers I was going to have to get them myself. I was enough of a realist to know that it was quite unlikely that one newspaper reporter was going to be able to solve a mystery that was obviously baffling an entire police force. I never expected to lay hands on the killer, I just wanted to know what the mystery was all about.

I drove to the Woodman Park Drive apartment complex hopeful that someone there would be able to tell me what kind of neighbor Barbara Butler had been. I parked on the shoulder of a circular road inside the complex of two-bedroom and townhouse-style apartments and walked over to the pool to see what was going on in the recreation area that Barbara Butler had left three days before to go to the store and die. The pool area was enclosed by a ten-foot wire fence that had obviously been built to keep out nonresidents without pool passes. I leaned up against the fence and looked through it, letting my eyes wander over the concrete apron of the pool as I wondered which spot was the exact spot where Barbara always sunbathed. It was a warm, sunny Saturday afternoon and the pool area was crowded with swimmers and sunbathers. They all had the look of un-marrieds-under-thirty. Several young men were having a game of water football; several young girls appeared sound asleep as they worked on their tans; no one seemed frightened; no one seemed to care that one of his or her former cotenants and poolside regulars was on an embalming table being prepared for burial.

I left the pool area and went to the rental office. I asked for and received directions to the neighborhood of the former Butler-Gray apartment. Then several complex employees offered these opinions about Barbara, Donna, and their apartment:

"The Butler girl was an all-round nice girl. . . . She looked like what you would think a nice schoolteacher would look like. . . . She was the kind of girl you would want your own daughter to be . . . very quiet, very friendly . . . pretty too . . . I heard they found a pair of sunglasses on her body . . . I never saw her with glasses on."

"Miss Butler and Miss Gray—both of them were just too nice; every time you saw them, they had a nice word. . . . Poor Miss Gray, she was sobbing uncontrollably the night they found the body. . . . I remember asking her if she

22

didn't want a friend to come stay with her. Donna answered, 'We don't have many friends around here.' "

"The two girls lived in apartment 9 since January. They moved from another apartment they'd been in from September to January—had a problem with the water in the other apartment, they said. . . . Their apartment wasn't wild at all. . . . The lease was in Barbara's name. . . . She had another girl who was going to move in with her after Miss Gray left."

I left the rental office and began walking toward the former Butler-Gray apartment. En route I encountered a young man in the act of moving a sprinkling hose from one section of new grass to another. I judged him to be an apartment-complex employee. I asked him if he had known Barbara Butler.

"You're either a cop or a reporter," he replied, with a sneering look on his face. "I can smell your kind a mile away and I won't talk to you unless I have to!"

"I'm a reporter. You don't have to talk to me, but why don't you want to?"

"Because of what the cops did to me and what you guys wrote about me when my fireworks experiment backfired and all those kids got hurt. I was just tryin' to put a little excitement into the graduation exercises but you bastards made it sound like I was tryin' to blow up the school."

I moved on, shaking my head and thinking: Strange . . . strange man.

Barbara Butler and Donna Gray had resided at 4957 Woodman Park Drive, apartment 9. I found 4957 Woodman Park Drive to be a block of ten townhouses located about a tenth of a mile north of the pool area. The ten townhouses had been constructed in sidewall-to-sidewall and back-wall-to-backwall rows of five houses each. Thus each townhouse had only one door—a front door. The turquoise front door of apartment 9—and the doors of the other four apartments in the same row—faced on a hidden courtyard. The courtyard was also an unpaved parking lot. It was enclosed, except for breezeways at three corners and a driveway at the fourth, by four blocks of townhouses.

I wanted to talk to the victim's neighbors. I knocked on the door of apartment 10, 4957 Woodman Park Drive—the address of Sally Kemper (a pseudonym) and Loretta Carmody, the nurse who had discovered the Volkswagen in the Ontario Store lot. There was no response to my knocks. The venetian blinds of the apartment were drawn and all was quiet.

I don't know why I went next door and knocked on the door of the former Butler-Gray apartment. I knew there was no one in that apartment. A little girl came skipping along the sidewalk, saw me standing on the doorstep of the apartment, stopped, and said, "Miss Butler doesn't live there any more, mister. She was awful pretty, but she got killed. I couldn't sleep last night."

I went on to apartment 8 and encountered two young men. One of them said, "We just moved in four days ago. We never met the dead girl and don't know anything about her."

Another neighbor pointed to apartment 9 and whispered, "The police were there again last night for a long time. I've heard talk that the poor girl was killed right there in that apartment."

I wondered. I stood in the dirt parking lot and stared at apartment 9. I wanted to get a firm impression in my mind of the two-story, white, wooden-front townhouse. There was a large window on the ground floor to the left of the door. An aerial—it appeared to be a television extension aerial—ran from the ground-floor window to a second-story window directly above. I listened to a rhythmic tapping sound caused by a breeze brushing the extension aerial against the front wall of the apartment and wondered if the two girls had slept well on windy nights. I paced off the distance from the edge of the parking lot to the door of the apartment; my size 13 shoes covered the distance in five walking-gait steps. If Barbara Butler's Volkswagen was parked right in front of her door, I thought, it wouldn't have been much of a problem to lug her body out of that apartment and into the car.

I walked along the edge of the parking lot until I came to the driveway leading into it from Woodman Park Drive. I stared at the asphalt driveway. The asphalt had the jet-black look of fresh pavement. A yellow rolling machine was parked alongside the driveway. Several sawhorses, often used to block off roads when paving work is in prog-ress, were stacked next to the rolling machine. My mind clicked into gear and raced away, adding up facts, asking questions, and making assumptions: Fresh asphalt . . . fresh tar . . . tar and oil splatterings on the undercar-riage, wheels and fenders of Butler's Volkswagen . . . Was this driveway being paved the day that the girl died? If so, did she get all of that tar on her car just from driving over this driveway on her way to the store? She could have seen the tar in daylight and probably would have driven around it. . . . She wouldn't even have had to have seen it . . . the driveway would have been blocked off until the tar was firm enough to drive on . . . but at night . . . when the tar and stones might still be loose enough to splatter . . . when somebody driving that car and body back to the parking lot couldn't see the tar . . .

I reined in my mind. Hell, the cops aren't stupid. They would have checked this out.

Still, I had to be certain. I doubted that the Kettering police would tell me anything, but I thought I knew somebody who would talk on an off-the-record basis if I could reach him at his home.

I went to a phone and called a coroner's investigator. He told me that paving work on the driveway was in progress on the day of Barbara Butler's disappearance. But, he added, "You're barking up the wrong tree if you think that the oil and tar on her car means that the victim returned to her apartment from the store and then got murdered. The tar and oil splatterings were on the car before the day of the murder."

In explanation the investigator told me these facts:

Barbara Butler had been an eighth-grade science teacher at Fairborn Central Junior High School from September of 1967 until June of 1968. (Fairborn is a northeast Dayton suburb of 35,000 and the site of Wright Patterson Air Force Base.) Sometime in the spring of 1968 Miss Butler accepted a position to teach computer programming at the National Cash Register Company's headquarters in Dayton. Her resignation as a schoolteacher took effect at the end of the school year on Wednesday, June 5. Miss Butler planned to start on her new job at NCR on July 1. After the close of school Miss Butler visited her parents at their home in Westerville. While she was at home Miss Butler complained about the oil and tar on her car and pointed the splatterings out to her father. Miss Butler left her parents' home on Tuesday, June 11, and returned to her Dayton-area apartment that evening. When she left her apartment for the store on the following afternoon, she did not have to drive over the freshly paved driveway because her car was *not* parked in the lot in front of her apartment door at this time—it was parked in another lot some distance away from her apartment. None of Miss Butler's neighbors could recall seeing her Volkswagen parked in the lot in front of her apartment at any time on Wednesday, June 12.

I accepted the investigator's explanation and apologized for having disturbed him at home needlessly. "I guess I've got too much imagination," I said.

"Don't apologize," the investigator replied. "I was thinking along the same lines myself, at first. . . . Now let me tell you about the tape on the victim's forearms. The tape wasn't just wound around her arms—it was put on very neatly, one loop at a time. We think that the arms were taped together behind the victim's back. But there is no way to tell for sure that the arms were behind her back. It is possible that the forearms were taped together in the form of a cross up against her chest. Now, what kind of people are taught to tape forearms together like that?"

"People who prepare bodies for delivery to a morgue?"

"Correct . . . Nurses have to be prepared to do things like that sometimes, don't they?"

"Nurses? Butler's two neighbors are nurses! They were at the pool with her . . . one of them found the body!"

"Look, I'm not saying that a neighbor killed the girl." The investigator shut me off. "I'm not saying that the girl was killed by someone that she knew—even if statistics tell us that is the case in about 90 percent of all homicides. I'm saying this: I've been in police work for nearly twenty-five years and when I can't find out anything wrong with a person—bells ring! I'm very suspicious of Mr. Good Guy because nobody is perfect. Take the Butler girl—she didn't smoke, she didn't drink, she didn't stay out late. . . . Well, she didn't sit home and just knit, either."

I decided that I had to make another attempt to talk to the two nurses. They had not responded to knocks on their door. I wondered if they would respond to a ringing phone. I looked up Loretta Carmody's number in the phone book and dialed it. A girl's voice answered. I identified myself and asked, "May I speak to Miss Carmody, please?"

"Speaking."

"Miss Carmody, I want to do a feature story about Barbara Butler. I wonder if you would take some time to talk with me about her?"

"I've said it all; you just check with the police."

The next thing I heard was a click; she had hung up.

I checked with the Kettering police on Loretta Carmody and her roommate, Sally Kemper. A Kettering lieutenant insisted that "neither girl is a suspect at this time." Then he asked me, "Why are you suspicious of the two nurses? Are you hurt because they won't talk to you? They've told us everything that they know. Don't you think they might be afraid to talk to you because they are scared and don't want their names in the paper?"

"Maybe so," I said, "but we've already pinpointed their address in print. I don't think they're scared of a killer finding them. I think they're scared to tell their story any more than they have to."

Barbara Butler studied for four years to be a schoolteacher and then she resigned a schoolteaching position less than one year after her 1967 graduation from the school of education at Miami University of Ohio. I wondered why.

A fellow teacher at Fairborn Central Junior High School explained, "They offered her more money at NCR and things like three trips a year, all expenses paid. She would have been crazy not to go there."

Her principal said, "She told me two weeks before the end of the school year that she would not be back in the fall. I was disappointed. She was an excellent teacher."

A former classmate said, "She told me that she always wanted to be a teacher. But her attitude changed about the middle of the school year: she guessed that she wasn't cut out for teaching children. Maybe it had something to do with the fact that many of her girl students looked older than she did. Barbara was just a little girl herself and didn't use much makeup—just lipstick and some eye shadow. She was very embarrassed on a field trip when a man came up to the class and asked, 'Which one is the teacher?' "

A pupil said, "She told us [the class] that she was quitting a long time before school was out. She was really fun and would yell at us; but we would kid with her and she would laugh with us. We loved her; all her students did—that's why we took up a collection to send flowers for her funeral."

I was confused and tired. I was not at all sure what kind of girl Barbara Butler was. I worked for a family

27

newspaper. I wrote a story about a nice girl who was "not the bar-going type."

John Nichols, a *Daily News* reporter, had some copies of the victim's picture made. He handed me one, saying, "This picture may be useful to you if you're going to keep digging on the Butler case. You may want to show it to people when you are asking questions about the victim."

On Sunday, June 16, the victim's remains were shown to her family and friends. "It was awful at the funeral home," a mourner sighed, "for the family, I mean: her dad isn't well; her mom, I felt so sorry for her—she couldn't bring herself to look in the coffin; and her brother Greg—he's in the service and had to get emergency leave—was terribly shook up. What a nice young man that Greg is—just as nice as his poor dead sister was."

Kettering police reported that "a considerable amount of information has come in from citizens and it is being checked out. We have begun to reinterview and we intend to go back over and over with different officers hoping that they can pull out something new. We have no suspects."

On Monday, June 17, Miss Barbara Ann Butler was buried in a small rural cemetery near her home town of Westerville.

Detective Lieutenant Albert J. Horn said in Kettering that morning that the "fingerprint evidence is still incomplete. A number of people got in the car after the discovery of the body, and we will have to eliminate all of their prints before we know what we have. Today is a day of organization. Four detective sergeants and myself are assigned to the case. It's a first of its kind for us—considering all the mystery around. All of the people connected with this case are strangers to us," he added, "none of them live in Kettering."

I thought: What the hell is going on? The case is in its fourth day and these suburban cops aren't even sure yet what kind of fingerprint evidence they've got. A day of organization for what? To bury the case right along with the girl's body?

5

The white letters on the blue sign at the town limits informed: "WESTERVILLE . . . Here Lived Benjamin R. Hanby Who Wrote Darling Nelly Gray."

The small town of 7,011 inhabitants located ten miles northeast of Columbus was also the seat of Otterbein College, founded there in 1847 by the Evangelical United Brethren Church.

Barbara Butler was a 1963 graduate of Westerville High School. The 1963 yearbook indicated that she was a very active high school student: she was in fourteen activities including the drama group, drill team, glee club, and the athletic association. Her yearbook portrait showed a smiling, dark-haired girl with bangs combed down over the forehead; pretty enough to be elected winter homecoming princess in her senior year. "Barbie Doll . . . Turn those lights off" was printed beside her picture.

Bob Shade, Barbara Butler's junior-year American history teacher, remembered her so well that he could stand at the front of an empty classroom six years later, point to the first desk in the third row, and say, "She sat right there. Near the close of school every year, I look over my students and try to visualize what they might be and do in life. I thought Barbie would make somebody a nice wife and mother someday. Whoever did this awful thing deprived somebody of a wonderful homemaker. She was bright, soft-spoken, very neat, and from a good home. I've read and reread the newspaper accounts of her death. But it is still unbelievable to me that such a thing could have happened. This got to me a lot more than did any of the recent national tragedies. [The assassination of Martin Luther King took place the preceding April and the murder of Robert F. Kennedy occurred one week prior to Miss Butler's death.] I keep asking myself, 'Why?' "

Many people must have felt as Bob Shade did about Barbara Butler's strange death. Her grave, in Blendon Central Cemetery, which, a sign stated, was "established on this site in 1830," was blanketed, in the days following her funeral, by a huge mound of fading red, pink, yellow, brown, and white flowers.

Ruth Trenton (a pseudonym), a high school classmate, said, "I'll always remember her sweet nature. You just can't think of Barbie without thinking something sweet. Everybody says nice things about the dead. But Barbie really was a great girl—I never heard anyone say anything bad about her. She had lots of dates with nice boys in school. Whenever she went out on a date, her mother would turn on all the porch lights. That interfered with a good-night kiss, so we always kidded her by saying, 'Turn off those lights.' The person who killed her had to be somebody who didn't know her because nobody could get that mad at Barbie Butler."

A former boyfriend recalled Barbara as "a quiet type of girl from a fellow's point of view—hard to get to know. She definitely wanted to be a wife and mother; but she was not looking around for a husband. It had to be the right person. If someone forcibly picked her up, it wouldn't have fazed her. She would know he was doing wrong and and wouldn't try to humor him . . . she would antagonize him. She would definitely stand up for what she believed in. And her beliefs were so pure. She wasn't sexually molested, so I don't believe she was killed by a sex maniac. But this is what bothers me—I just can't imagine her having an enemy in the world."

Barbara Butler's parents, Mr. and Mrs. Bernard Butler, resided in a brick ranch home with attached two-car garage. It was a neighborhood of large homes and spacious, well-kept lawns, many of them dotted with huge evergreen trees that created what was almost a "deep woods" atmosphere. A resident boasted, "This is a fine neighborhood—everybody minds their own business. I didn't even know that the Butler girl was living away from home until I read in the paper that she was murdered."

Bernard Butler operated a Columbus dry-cleaning establishment. He said his daughter appeared "normal and untroubled" during the days she spent in the family home following the close of school and preceding the murder. Mrs. Butler said that Barbara was still sleeping when she left the house to play golf about 9:00 A.M. on the morning of Tuesday, June 11. When Mrs. Butler returned from her golf outing in the afternoon Barbara had already begun her last eighty-mile drive back to her suburban Dayton apartment. She made two stops on the way: at her father's dry-cleaning plant to pick up some clothing and at a Columbus department store to visit a girlfriend.

Mrs. Joan Sullivan Denton (a pseudonym), a sales clerk at the department store, told me that she was Barbara Butler's "best home-town girlfriend." She said that her brother, Mark Sullivan (a pseudonym), was the boyfriend that Miss Butler had unsuccessfully sought the pool pass for on the day of her death. Mrs. Denton also revealed that Miss Butler visited her at the store not once but twice on the days immediately preceding her death.

"She stopped by to see me the first time on Monday, June 10," Mrs. Denton said. "Barb came to the store that day to look for some furniture that she would be needing for her apartment after Donna Gray moved out and took her stuff with her. I saw her the second time about four o'clock on the afternoon of Tuesday, June 11. She said that she was on her way back to Dayton, and had just stopped in to exchange some powder. She told me, 'I'll be seeing your brother in Dayton this weekend and then we're going up to Maumee [a suburb of Toledo] for a few days next week.'"

I asked Mrs. Denton this question: "Did Barbara seem upset or worried about anything when you talked to her last week?"

"Yes, she did and I think that the police should know about it," Mrs. Denton answered.

"Tell me," I said.

Then Joan Sullivan Denton told this story:

"On Monday Barbara talked a great deal about a problem that she had had with some former pupils. She said that there were these boys in one of her classes who resented her for trying to get them to use their potential. She would talk to them, you know, get after them to use their brains. But they wouldn't. So she flunked them. Then they moved her car. She was very upset about that because it was her first car and she took great care of it. She picked it out herself in Europe last summer on her college-graduation trip. She told me she contacted the police and wanted to prosecute those boys for moving her car. She thought they had damaged her car. She quit teaching because of the attitude of her students. She told me she saw too much in the younger generation that she didn't like.

She said, 'I'm tired of playing around with eighth graders.' "

"Are you trying to tell me that you think she was killed by some students?"

"I don't know about that. I do know that a lot of people at the funeral were talking about those boys being hateful to Barbie. Somebody said that they threatened to get even with her if she reported them to the police for moving her car. I also know this: the person who killed Barbie would have had to surprise her. If a stranger came up to her in that parking lot, she would either turn and walk away or get in her car and lock the door."

Then Mrs. Denton asked me, "Why didn't the police find Barbara's car sooner than they did? Her roommate Donna got scared and gave out the wrong license number; she gave out the 1967 registration number instead of the 1968 license. But the description of the car was right. Another thing, why haven't the police contacted either myself or my brother?"

6

The police and municipal offices of the city of Kettering are located in an old white stone building that, in June of 1968, appeared sorely in need of a good white-wash job. The building would have been sizable as a school-house, which, from appearances, was probably its original function. As a city hall–police station it was small and crowded with functionaries. The police occupied half of the ground floor and all of the basement.

Kettering's eight detectives—Lieutenant Albert Horn, four sergeants and three men with the grade of detective—worked out of a cramped two-room office in the basement. I went there on the morning of Wednesday, June 19, to get some answers to the questions raised by Joan Sullivan Denton.

I asked, "What do you know about a problem that the victim had with some of her pupils?"

A detective answered, "We have been aware that Miss

Butler had a problem at school. We intend to check it out with school authorities."

"I understand that the wrong license number was given out on the missing-person report. Can you tell me why this happened and what effect it had on police attempts to locate the girl?"

"We feel that it was an honest error made by a very frightened girl. Miss Gray was apparently so confused on the night of her roommate's disappearance that she gave the Mad River Township officer the 1967 registration number as the 1968 number. A Kettering officer located a 1967 silver-blue Volkswagen bearing tag number 8771NN (Miss Butler's correct 1968 registration number) in the Ontario Store lot some time before the actual discovery of the body. The officer turned away when he noted that the license number on the Volkswagen did not correspond with the information he had regarding the license number of the car of a missing Mad River Township girl."

"Why haven't you talked to either Joan Denton or her brother, Mark Sullivan?"

"We intend to talk to them as the investigation widens. Right now we are just a small-town police force without a suspect in a murder case of wide interest. We don't have the manpower to do all the things we would like to be doing—it's very time-consuming just checking out leads provided by the general public."

"What are you doing to find a suspect?"

"We have completed fingerprinting all of the persons known to have been inside the Volkswagen after the discovery of the body. We have eliminated all of these persons' prints from our evidence. We now have several strange partial finger and palm prints for which we have no matches. We are sending these prints, along with other evidence found in the car, to the FBI laboratory in Washington for analysis."

At that moment I didn't know whom I felt sorrier for: the murder victim or the murder investigators. The Kettering police were saying very little about their investigation and the little they did say made the situation seem all the more pathetic.

I went to my newspaper and told Managing Editor Greg Favre and City Editor Doug Walker what the Kettering police had told me. It was decided that Miss Butler's "problem" at school was worthy of extensive exploration. Reporters were sent to the school and obtained two somewhat different views of an incident that apparently centered on an alleged damaging of Miss Butler's Volkswagen by several pupils.

Principal Robert Martin said, "Miss Butler's car and those of several other teachers were moved around last spring in the school parking lot—one being placed on a nearby sidewalk. It was a prank done by three boys I could class as troublemakers and there was nothing unusual about it. None of these boys were among the seven failures in Miss Butler's eighth-grade science classes. Miss Butler reported the incident to me. But her car was not damaged. Her reaction seemed sweet and pleasant and that was the last I heard of the incident. Miss Butler did have previous trouble with a thirteen-year-old boy who was not involved in the car-moving incident."

A teacher who indicated that she was a close faculty friend of Miss Butler's said, "She was hysterical about the moving of her car. She thought the transmission had been damaged. She said, 'That's it, I've had it.' But at the end of the day she had calmed down somewhat. I believe it would be wise for the police to talk to a thirteen-year-old boy named Eddie Allen [a pseudonym]. He treated Barbara very rudely and insulted and upset her several times during the closing weeks of school. He is just a puny boy and not what I would call fast; but I've heard that his family has sought psychiatric help for him. He was transferred out of Barbara's class into another class taught by a male teacher."

I returned to the Kettering police and told them what the principal and teacher had said. A Kettering detective seemed unimpressed. He brushed me off with these words: "There is nothing further for us to pursue through the Fairborn school system at this time. We have been told that a boy out there had heated words with Miss Butler several times near the close of school. However, the boy and his family moved away right after the close of school. They were gone before the murder. We still have nothing to go on—no motives."

I went with another reporter to the thirteen-year-old boy's home. We found him and his mother very much *not* moved away from the area. We were told by the mother, "I can't let you talk to my son. He is quite upset over Miss Butler—he feels he may have said some things to her that

34

he now wishes he hadn't. My son had difficulties with Miss Butler in class, but the difficulties had nothing to do with her personally. It was the course—he has had problems in science courses before and prefers a male teacher for science."

I thought that I had been getting the runaround. I went back to the Kettering police and stated my feelings:

"You people say you can't find anybody with a motive for killing Barbara Butler. Then some reporters scratch around and find a kid who apparently hated the girl. You tell us that the kid couldn't have killed Butler because he had moved away before the murder. Well, the kid didn't move away! I just saw him—with my own eyes—hiding behind his mother's apron strings while she was admitting that the boy had a problem with Butler and is too upset about some of the names he called her to talk about her now. I want to know why you're so damned certain that that kid couldn't have killed his teacher."

"We assume that the unidentified partial finger and palm prints found in the Volkswagen are those of the killer," Lieutenant Horn began his explanation. "The prints have been analyzed and it has been determined that the prints were made by a large male hand. [There is no absolute way to determine sex by fingerprint analysis. However, the ridges on a female print are usually smaller and closer together than were the ridges on the unidentified partial prints found in the Volkswagen.] The boy has small hands, so the prints, obviously, are not Eddie Allen's. We would still be willing to suspect the boy if he could have had any prior knowledge that Miss Butler was going to the Ontario Store on Wednesday, June 12. But we have found out that Barbara Butler didn't know herself that she was going to the store until just before she went—it was a spur-of-the-moment thing. Without knowing where Barbara Butler was going to be, the boy would have had to have taken a car, driven down to that lot and met her accidentally outside the store. The victim almost had to have met her killer in that lot, because she said nothing about meeting anyone or going anywhere except to the store. We just can't see the boy meeting her there under those circumstances."

The detective's explanation was logical; but the case was so illogical that I felt that I had to keep the boy, Eddie Allen, in my thoughts alongside the roommate and the two nurses; none of them, I thought, could be fully eliminated. And what about the boyfriend who was coming for the weekend? Had his sister purposely steered me onto a trail that would lead to suspicion of the thirteen-year-old boy instead of her brother?

I phoned Mark Sullivan—who had apparently had a dual close association with Barbara Butler: boyfriend and brother of her best girlfriend. Mark told me that he "had an off-and-on dating relationship with Barbara for five years." He said he considered her to be "the finest girl I've ever known and the most wonderful girl I've ever dated."

Sullivan then told this story:

"I phoned Barb at her apartment about ten-thirty or eleven o'clock on Tuesday [June 11]. My reason for calling was to see if everything was still on for the weekend. She said yes. I had a date with Barbie two weeks before and we had decided, then, that I would come to Dayton on Friday [June 14]. I don't know where I was going to stay; she said she would make the arrangements. Then on Sunday she was going to come to Toledo and stay at the home of a friend of mine's fiancée. We joked on the phone and laughed. She said she was going to get a barbecue because I was coming down. She told me she had just gotten back from Westerville and had talked with my sister, Joan, in the store that afternoon. If she had anything bothering her, she would have said something. Nothing in the world was wrong.

"Then Thursday night, about eight-thirty or nine o'clock, her roommate, Donna Gray, called me and told me to 'sit down.' She said she had some bad news for me. She then told me Barb had been killed. I asked, 'Was she in an auto accident?' She said, 'No, foul play.' I'm not sure how Donna Gray got my phone number. I never met her until the Friday after Barb was killed."

Donna Gray's whereabouts and actions at the time of Barbara Butler's disappearance and death were a mystery to everyone except her family, close friends, and the Kettering police. Reporters made several attempts to locate her in order to learn her story, but could not penetrate the veil of secrecy and obscurity in which she had surrounded herself: she had not employed a commercial hauler to move her possessions from the Dayton to the Columbus area . . . the telephone company and utility company had no Columbus listing for her . . . even officials at Ohio State University, where Miss Gray was known to be taking a postgraduate course at a summer-school session, would not reveal her Columbus address or her schedule.

One afternoon in late June *Daily News* police reporter Denny Gilbert went to the Ohio State campus determined to find Miss Gray. Gilbert, then single and a handsome young man in his early twenties, began his search at the registrar's office. He did not identify himself or his mission but, instead, began to flirt with a secretary. The young woman was receptive to Gilbert's advances and he was able to con her into looking up Donna Gray's schedule. Gilbert learned that Miss Gray was taking a course in evolutionary biology and should have been, at that moment, in room 110 of the dentistry building. He rushed to the classroom building, brushing against a thin young woman on his way in the doorway. He went to room 110 and found the classroom empty. He made several inquiries about the building for Miss Gray but learned nothing. He returned to the registrar's office and asked his secretary friend for Miss Gray's Columbus address. The girl said she could not risk taking a second peek into the files. Gilbert left Columbus feeling defeated because, as he said on his return to Dayton, "I couldn't even find out what Gray looks like."

That night I was in bed and sound asleep when the noises of a ringing phone began to bring me back toward consciousness. My wife, Charlotte, turned on a bedroom light and answered the phone. A moment later she handed the phone to me saying, "Bill, it's some cop—he says he has to talk to you, right now!"

I took the phone and—still only half awake—said, "Hello," to Kettering Detective Sergeant Jim Tobias.

He sounded excited. "Sorry to call you at this hour," he apologized, "but I have to ask you this question: Did the *Daily News* have a young reporter in Columbus today looking for Donna Gray?"

"Yes. Denny Gilbert."

"Oh, good. Would you describe Gilbert to me, please?"

"Young, very good looking, with dark curly hair . . ."

"That's good enough," the detective said with a sigh. "It fits in with the description that Miss Gray gave us."

"What are you talking about, sergeant? What's going on?"

"Your man Gilbert really put Miss Gray in a panic. She

thought the assailant was stalking the campus after her."

"Why would she think that?"

"I can't explain. But you might ask Gilbert if he remembers bumping into a girl over at Ohio State. You also might advise him not to pull a stunt like that again—Donna has the campus police on alert for him."

The detective hung up.

I turned to my wife and said, "Those cops are cracking up . . . calling me in the middle of the night and asking me to describe Denny Gilbert. Butler's roommate is obviously scared of her own shadow. . . . Why?"

My wife snapped off the bedroom light and said, "It sounds to me like you're the one who's cracking up. When are you going to forget that murder case, so we can start living like human beings again?"

I wondered what life at Miami University had been like for Barbara Butler and went to the campus, located some thirty-five miles southwest of Dayton at Oxford, to find out.

The yearbook wasn't much help: a few agate lines informed me that she was a biology major and had taken part in only two campus activities—the student education association and house council (a women's disciplinary organization). From other sources I learned that she had lived in women's residence halls throughout her college career and that she and Donna Gray lived in the same dormitory during their sophomore year (Miss Gray transferred to Ohio State for her junior and senior years).

There was no file on Barbara Butler at the student counseling service, which indicated that she had had no serious problems in college. "She just came here and graduated," a counselor said. "There's nothing outstanding either way —good or bad—in her record or her activities here."

A former classmate said, "She was one of many faces in a crowd. I guess she was the type you would remember only if you sat next to her in class."

Dr. Paul M. Daniels said, "I had Miss Butler two years—for methods of teaching biology and vertebrate zoology. She was a fine young lady and a slightly above average student—far from the bottom and not the top of the class. She had to work hard for her grades and did. She was the kind of girl you would think of as the last to get into any kind of trouble."

Tests run at the time of autopsy had eliminated alcohol and carbon monoxide as factors in Miss Butler's death. "Her carbon monoxide level of less than 5 percent," Coroner's Chief Investigator Harry Bloomer said, "could be the result of her being in a small, closed area—such as the Volkswagen—with someone smoking a cigarette or from being in a car that was following close behind a truck with a bad exhaust. If she had actually smoked a cigarette, her carbon monoxide level would be about 10 percent."

The presence of drugs as an incapacitating factor remained a strong possibility for the first two weeks of the investigation. Then on Friday, June 28, the coroner's office revealed the results of tissue study tests: Miss Butler's blood barbiturate level was negative. "That rules out all drugs," Bloomer said, "except 'speed' or LSD. Additional acid extraction tests are in progress in an attempt to determine the presence of 'speed.' There is no known test for the presence of LSD."

Jayne Ellison is a living contradiction of the idea that a female's place in journalism is the society department. Jayne could do and say anything that a man was capable of—and did. She loved to tell of a time early in her newspaper career when she was a Columbus, Ohio, police reporter: she went to the scene of a reported disturbance, entered a house, encountered a body and its hysterical murderer—and calmly talked him into coming outside to meet the police. In Mexico during World War II she met John Steinbeck and entered upon a friendship that lasted until his death. Although she was a divorcée living alone in a farmhouse, she reacted to a middle-of-the-night telephoned threat by telling the caller, "C'mon out and see me anytime—the door's never locked, but . . . I got a loaded rifle and my aim is good."

In June of 1968 Jayne Ellison was the medical writer for the Dayton *Daily News*. She had numerous contacts among experts in criminal psychiatry and used them to obtain these opinions of the type of person who killed Barbara Ann Butler:

Dr. Joseph J. Trevino, a former director of the Ohio Mental Hygiene and Correction Department's psychiatric criminology program, who at the time was a private practitioner in Piqua (a community of twenty thousand located twenty-five miles north of Dayton), said:

"I would strongly suspect that the killer is a compulsive personality because of the careful arrangement of the girl's clothing under the body, the placing of the blanket over the body and, then, the final act of putting the sunglasses on top. Emotionally this person is very ill and probably someone who knew the victim more than casually. The only other possibility, considering the absence of any indication of a struggle or the presence of drugs, is that the girl might have been very scared—hysterical, in fact—and could not move. Strangulation is an awful sensation and the girl would have struggled unless she was in a deep sleep or coma. The neat manner in which the arms were taped indicates that more than one person was involved or that the tape was put on while the girl was unconscious."

Dr. Henry Luidens, a former superintendent of the Lima, Ohio, State Hospital for the criminally insane, took a different view:

"My choice is that this is a transient or itinerant killing and that the crime will be repeated with remarkable similarities. There should be a check made of major cities to see if any other parking-lot deaths have occurred which might indicate a pattern of such crimes. The fastidiousness is most significant. Despite the crime, there seems to have been a great reverence for the girl. The placement of the clothing should be considered a last act of dignity, the most bizarre final act. There was no sexual molestation, but this should be considered a crime of a sexual nature. It is not infrequent that the objective of the sexual pervert can be obtained way short of the normal act."

Dr. Lowell K. Cunningham, head of the Chillicothe, Ohio, Treatment and Research Center, said:

"The killer is apparently someone of better than average intelligence who was not thinking clearly at the time . . . and someone reasonably well known to the victim. An attempt was made to be complex and confusing. . . . The person is likely quite resourceful because of the use of things at hand, such as the blanket, to cover the body. With the long hours between the fixed time of death and discovery of the body, it suggests that the body was put in the car either in a garage or under cover of darkness."

7

As June began to wane, the words of a Kettering detective painted a picture of ebbing hopes that the murder of Barbara Ann Butler could ever be solved. "We haven't turned up a thing," he said, "and there's nothing on the horizon. It's always possible that something could come in from left field. We're still hoping that the FBI will be able to tell us something from their analysis of the evidence. But if we don't catch him or her or it, we'll at least have a folderful of notes to prove that we tried."

Many of my coworkers at the *Daily News* felt that the investigation had failed simply because it had been conducted by a small suburban police department unaccustomed to the handling of complicated homicides. I thought that this was a factor in the killer's ability to remain at large. But there was more to it than that. Sometimes I thought that everything about the whole affair was ill-starred. So many improbable things had happened: a girl had walked out the door of a suburban store on one afternoon . . . her body had been found in the store parking lot the next . . . she had been strangled with some type of cord that didn't leave marks all the way around her neck . . . there was tar on her car and tar on her apartment-house driveway, but one plus one equaled nothing . . . the body had been left nude but had not been sexually molested . . . the body had been jammed down so far and covered so neatly that its presence could not be noted by a person standing next to the car and looking in through a window . . . the roommate had given out the wrong license number when she reported the girl missing . . . a police officer had found the car and left without doing anything when the license number did not match . . . a friend of the victim had come to the lot later and encouraged a store employee to force the car open and discover the body . . . shoppers and police had gotten into the car and disturbed evidence . . . the roommate had gone into hiding and the neighbors would not talk . . . the victim's friends who would talk pictured her as a goddess of goodness . . . only one person was known to have expressed hatred for the victim and he was a thirteen-year-old boy whom the police refused to suspect.

It was all so complicated and so wrong—but I knew that there had to be an answer to it somewhere. In the early days of the investigation I learned comparatively little from questioning Kettering police. The attitude of the police was personally frustrating, but understandable considering the position they were in: a suburban police department accustomed to solving unpublicized minor crimes suddenly entrusted with the solution of a mysterious, highly publicized murder. The police apparently took the attitude that every fact of the case which appeared in print was a fact lost to the investigation. So they kept silent about as many aspects of the case as they could until the passage of time dulled both the usefulness of these facts to themselves and the news value of them to me as a reporter. As the trail to the killer grew colder in early July, the police provided some answers about areas of the case for which I had many questions:

Q. No one knows where Barbara Butler went after she went out the door of that store. What did her friends expect her to be doing on the evening of Wednesday, June 12?

A. She told the neighbor nurses and her roommate that she was going to stay home and strip the wax off the kitchen floor and clean up the apartment in preparation for the arrival of the boyfriend, Mark Sullivan, that weekend.

Q. Mark Sullivan—he is not in any way a suspect?

A. No. Who, besides the parents, would have more to lose by Barbara Ann Butler's death? She was apparently getting ready to give him a grand welcome.

Q. How does the roommate, Donna, account for her whereabouts and actions on June 12–13?

A. Donna Gray was at the school where she taught this past year, cleaning out her desk, on the afternoon of Wednesday, June 12. She returned to her apartment about 4:00 P.M. to meet her parents, who had driven down from their home for a visit. The parents and Donna had supper out in a restaurant and returned to the Butler-Gray apartment about 8:00 P.M. Donna was apparently quite upset when she found that Barbara was not home at this time; she said that she and Barbara always kept each other aware of their movements—by note if not by word of mouth. Miss

Gray made inquiries about Barbara around the apartment complex, learning from the nurses that Barbara had gone to the store that afternoon. Donna's parents, who are also schoolteachers, left her apartment about 9:30 P.M. to return to their home. Miss Gray called hospitals, friends, and then Miss Butler's parents in an attempt to get word of her. One of the nurses came over and, about 10:30 P.M., phoned a friend who is the wife of a Dayton police detective. The nurses explained the situation and asked the detective for advice. His first reaction was that there was nothing to worry about; there is nothing unusual about a single adult not being home by 10:30 at night. The nurse called back sometime later and the detective then advised her to contact the Mad River Township police.

Q. The missing-person report was received by Mad River police at 11:06 P.M. on Wednesday and an officer reported himself on the scene to begin taking missing-person information at 11:38 P.M. Isn't this unusually early for police to start "working" a missing-person complaint? Don't most police in this area wait seventy-two hours before acting on missing adults?

A. That is true for most larger departments—the feeling being that adults have the right to go and come as they please without telling anyone of their movements or whereabouts. But Mad River is a small department and acted immediately on the complaint.

Q. What did Donna Gray do after the Mad River officer left the apartment?

A. Apparently she became even more frightened than she had been earlier when she gave out the wrong license number. She phoned her parents about 2:30 A.M. and had them return to stay with her through the night. Then in the morning she summoned Miss Butler's parents from Westerville.

Q. Did she stay at the apartment all day?

A. She remained at the apartment with her parents until after the body was discovered. Then she went to her parents' home and spent the night there.

Q. Where were Miss Butler's parents when the body was discovered?

A. En route back to Westerville. Mr. Butler was not in the best of health at the time. Both parents had to be placed under sedation after they were notified of their daughter's fate.

Q. A neighbor nurse, Loretta Carmody, went to the store and found the car and body. Why didn't Donna Gray go to the store to search for Barbara?

A. Miss Gray was prepared to move out of the apartment that evening—Thursday, June 13. Miss Gray's fiancé was coming from Columbus with a U-haul trailer to move Miss Gray's belongings to her new apartment in Columbus. He was apparently going to get there when he could—there was no fixed arrival time—so Miss Gray felt that she had to remain at the old apartment to await his arrival. The body had been discovered and the investigation had begun before the fiancé appeared at the apartment. He had to return to Columbus with an empty trailer that night, then make another 160-mile round trip the next day to get Miss Gray's possessions after the apartment had been vacuumed, dusted for fingerprints, and inspected for any signs of a struggle having taken place there.

Q. I understand that fibers from the dress were found in the living room carpeting of Miss Butler's apartment. Are you certain that Barbara was not killed in her own apartment or next door at the nurses' apartment?

A. We went all through the Butler-Gray apartment and the neighbors' apartment. There was no indication that anything out of the ordinary had taken place in either apartment. We did find some fiber tatters in Miss Butler's apartment which matched fibers found on the floor mat of the death car. However, that didn't prove a thing because Miss Butler made the pant-dress in the apartment and the tatters were apparently in the carpeting as a result of her sewing.

Q. Do you believe Miss Butler was murdered in her Volkswagen?

A. Probably. The coroner has said that lividity indicates that the body was forced down onto the floor of the car immediately after death. But we have no idea where the car was at that time. This is just one of the factors in making this crime one of the most baffling and complicated on record. So many things are possible when there is no evidence to indicate where, how, or why the crime was committed. This is an extremely bizarre case. There is very little about it that makes sense. There have been times when we have thought this was not a homicide, but a suicide. The marks on the sides of the neck were like hanging marks.

Q. You don't seriously believe that Barbara Butler committed suicide?

A. We can't—the coroner has ruled it a homicide. But considering her death a suicide is not as outlandish as you might think. I've seen suicide victims who have tied their hands behind their backs and hanged themselves . . . at the last minute a natural urge to live causes them to break their bindings. Of course, in this case someone would have had to cut the body down, force it onto the floor of the car, cover the body, and drive the car back to the lot.

Q. Could the car have been driven with the body in the position in which it was found?

A. It would have been difficult and would have required a good deal of driving skill. We believe, however, that the car was driven—probably with the body in the position as found—because we cannot believe that the whole crime could have taken place unobserved in that busy parking lot. The girl had to have left the lot for at least some of the time between her disappearance and death. It is easier for us to believe that the victim left the lot alive in her own car, and then was returned to the lot dead in the same car. Thus the killer had to drive the car.

Q. When is the earliest time that the car could have been returned to the lot after the murder if, in fact, the car left the lot at all?

A. Sometime between 9:30 P.M. and 10:30 P.M. on Wednesday, June 12. Several people recall having seen the car on the lot that evening, but the witnesses differ about the time. We do not know where Barbara Butler parked when she went to the store. However, on Wednesday evening the car was seen in the same place it was when the body was discovered the next day—eleven parking spaces out from the store in the third row from the south extremity of the lot. This area of the lot is a section where store employees are told to park their cars. We have a witness who says the car was on the lot at 9:30 P.M. However, a store employee is certain that the car was not there when he left for home shortly after the store closed at 10:00 P.M. Another employee insists that he saw the car on the lot when he left for home about 10:30 P.M. No one recalls seeing the car on the lot prior to 9:30 P.M.

Q. The nurse who found the car—did she enter the car after the body was discovered?

A. Her prints were not found inside the car.

Q. I'd like to know about the finger and palm prints that you did find in the car. Can you tell me about them?

A. When we first looked in that car it appeared to be very clean. We didn't think that we would find any prints other than those belonging to people who got in the car after the discovery of the body. But when our print man started spreading his gook around, prints started popping up everywhere except the place that you might think you'd find the most prints: there were no prints on the steering wheel—just some smears. That could indicate that the killer either wore gloves or mopped up everything in the car that he could remember having touched. But Barbara Butler's prints were found in many places about the car. This indicated that the killer had not mopped up because he could only do this after she was dead and unable to leave fingerprints. Eventually we were able to identify and set aside all the fresh prints in the car except some smudges on the doors and door posts that we will never be able to identify and a partial fingerprint on the back of the rearview mirror (next to two prints identified as Miss Butler's) and a partial palm print on the outside of the driver's-side door. These partials will not match with any prints that we have on file or with any specimens of persons we have talked to in connection with this case.

Q. Is it true that the prints of several police officers were found inside that car?

A. Just between us girls: this case was screwed up right at the start. There are many things about the first hours of the investigation that we would like to be able to do over again.

Q. What about your other evidence?

A. To be honest, we can't make much of anything out of it. We've sent everything to the FBI in hopes that their experts will be able to tell us something—we'd especially like a match from the FBI files for our partial finger and palm prints. We assume that these partials belong to the killer. As you know, we have expert opinion that these partials are from a large male hand. We also think the killer is a man because it would have required a good deal of strength to rip that dress off the girl and force the body down onto the floor the way it was. The tampon beside the body was a weird thing—it was apparently pulled out of the girl. A man wouldn't normally do that, unless he was trying to do something else with his hand when he discovered the presence of the tampon and just jerked his hand out as part of a disgusted reaction. This might indicate that the killer is a big strong guy with a weak stomach. Even if we make that assumption, it still doesn't tell us much. And we can say the same thing about most of the other stuff found in the car. The tape is just common adhesive that can be purchased anywhere. As far as we know, it wasn't Miss Butler's—she didn't keep a first-aid kit in the car. It wasn't from the doctors' offices where the nurses worked, either—we checked. It's kind of hard to believe that the girl pulled her right arm free of the tape; it's more likely that the killer pulled the arm free after death to make it easier to get the dress off the body.

Q. But then you ask yourself: why was the dress ripped off? It would have been a lot easier to take it off by lowering the zipper, right?

A. Ripping the dress was probably a ruse. We think the killer did a lot of things to throw us off. We found several shades and lengths of human hair on the floor of the car; but we haven't been able to match them—none of them were from the victim. We found a brown string; it doesn't match with anything in Miss Butler's wardrobe—or her friends', either. The ashtrays of the car were overflowing with butts and ashes. Barbara Butler didn't smoke. Donna Gray says she thinks all those butts were hers; she smokes and apparently did a good deal of riding around with Barbara. There were piles of ashes on the driver's-side floor; but the lab can't tell if these ashes match with the ashes or the butts in the ashtrays. Maybe the killer smokes; and maybe he just put those ashes on the floor to make us think that he smokes—we just don't know. The yellow towel and the washcloth were in the car because a friend had left them there after swimming at the apartment pool. We can't make any sense at all of the small piece of blue terry cloth found in the shopping bag. It is interesting that all of the packages were found on the back seat, stacked to the right side as if they had been lifted into the car through the passenger-side door. It would have been easier for a little girl like Barbara to have just put that twenty-four-pound barbecue down on the front seat—unless there was someone there with her who was going to be sitting in the front seat.

Q. You have said publicly many times that you have

no suspects. Isn't it true that you had a very suspicious person in for questioning early in the investigation?

A. Last year a young woman was grabbed in the same Ontario Store lot and robbed at knife point by a young man. He was on probation at the time of the murder. We have questioned the man about Miss Butler's death and his story checks out.

Q. Have any of Miss Butler's friends or associates ever come under formal suspicion?

A. I can honestly tell you that the investigation has never centered on one particular individual who, to our knowledge, may have known or have had any prior acquaintance with Barbara Butler.

Q. Have any of Barbara Butler's friends taken polygraph examinations?

A. Yes—and they all passed, including the roommate and the two nurses. This was done as part of our reinterviewing process.

Q. Were these people questioned—rather than interviewed?

A. We started out determined to read a subject his rights before an interview turned into a questioning session. Recently a number of interviews have turned into questioning without mentioning Miranda (the 1966 United States Supreme Court decision requiring that suspects be advised of their rights to counsel and against self-incrimination before being questioned about a crime which they are suspected of having committed). We feel we are all right on this because the investigation has never centered on any one prime suspect.

Q. You have indicated to me that you do not believe that Barbara was killed by a prior associate. Do you feel, then, that her murder was unpremeditated?

A. You can't premeditate killing someone unless you know that they exist.

Q. Touché! But if the murder was not premeditated, then the killer didn't have a lot of time to plot out all these ruses we've been mentioning. Do you think that all of this confusion and mystery arose by chance?

A. The killer could be the luckiest bastard that ever lived.

Q. The victim wasn't raped. What does that mean to you?

A. The fact our girl was in her menstrual cycle may have cooled an attacker's ardor; he may have intended to

48

outstanding reputation in his community and among law-enforcement officers in the state of Ohio and the nation. He was named city employee of the year in 1960 and Kiwanis Club "Man of the Year" in 1966; he was elected president of the Ohio Association of Chiefs of Police in 1962 and a vice-president of the International Association of Chiefs of Police in 1965. (Under standard advancement procedure, Shryock became president of the International Association in the fall of 1970.) In 1967 Shryock was one of fifteen chiefs of police named to a national civil disorders study group. The chiefs toured cities with a history of racial disturbances and evaluated police capabilities, problems, and needs under such conditions in a report to President Johnson's commission on civil disorders. Under Shryock the Kettering Police Department increased in size from eleven officers to fifty-three; police pay tripled; and detective, traffic, records, and training units were established.

However, a policeman's lot is not always easy—even in suburban Kettering, where City Manager Ervin L. Welch said that the crime rate was "not up to the national average because we don't have the poverty, gambling, pawnshops, red lights, and skid rows." Some of Shryock's more difficult days there—at least from a monetary standpoint—were his first days on the job in 1955. His original appointment to the six-thousand-dollar-per-year job had to be rescinded after an attorney made an issue of a technicality that required Kettering's police chief to be a legal resident. Shryock was named safety director on an interim basis until he could establish residency; however, the village clerk refused to sign Shryock's pay check on the grounds that his appointment to the spurious post of safety director was illegal. Eventually the matter was settled amicably and Kettering police affairs were conducted efficiently and without serious incident until the 1960's—a time of trial, transition, and rising crime rates for policemen everywhere in the United States.

In 1963 the Kettering police clearance rate (percentage of cases solved) began to drop (from 46 percent in 1962, to 44 percent in 1963, and on down to a low of 28 percent in 1967). Police said that the decrease in efficiency was due to an increase in the crime rate and a lack of manpower. That year the Kettering force numbered only thirty-four men spread over three shifts. Police claimed that the force should have numbered ninety-five men to be in line with national averages for cities of comparable size to Kettering. Police

51

spokesmen warned that because of days off, sickness, vacations, and the need for some officers to perform dispatching and administrative tasks, their eighteen-square-mile city of 62,000 was often protected by a line operations force of only three patrolmen and one sergeant. Chief Shryock pointed to a 1963 incident which, he thought, emphasized his department's need for more officers. "Within a five-minute period one night," he said, "we received calls on a supermarket burglary, a fire requiring officers to reroute traffic, a personal-injury traffic accident, and a man chasing his wife with a shotgun. We should have responded to each call with two men. But we had only three policemen in the whole city. One officer went after the man with the shotgun, another went to the burglary, and the third policeman was assigned to the traffic accident. The firemen had to direct their own traffic."

Kettering City Manager Welch reacted to police pleas for more men by saying, "A massive use of manpower won't help solve the problem. We need moral rejuvenation—improved techniques and training." He agreed that "police activity has increased faster than we anticipated," but he claimed that the increase was due "not to major crime but to traffic, domestic problems, and juvenile delinquency." The manager thought that "expanding the city recreation program now might deflate the need for more policemen later."

The city administration's attitude led to a number of resignations from the police force, creating a situation in which the department was consistently four to six men under authorized strength. Officers who remained on the force began asking for higher pay and more fringe benefits. Police dissatisfaction eventually surfaced into a public dispute between the Kettering Fraternal Order of Police (FOP) and the city administration. The argument became so bitter at one point that Seregant Keith Thompson, the FOP president, charged that City Manager Welch threatened to fire the entire police force. Welch denied the accusation and countercharged that the police demands for higher pay, more officers, and increased fringe benefits would be met "only on the basis of supply and demand, not on militancy or pressure tactics."

In the fall of 1965 a daring burglar may have inadvertently supplied some pressure on behalf of police demands by breaking into sixteen homes in one of Kettering's most fashionable sections, taking only cash and high-value items, leaving no clues, and adding insult to his victims' sense of loss by leaving the taxpaying husbands' empty trousers on their front lawns.

In response to citizen demands for an "adequate force," the Kettering City Council met police pay demands and increased the authorized strength of the department to forty-six men. City Manager Welch admitted he was "under pressure to add as many more men to the force as we can afford."

In 1967 Kettering's major crime rate increased an alarming 34 percent. 3,324 criminal offenses were reported to Kettering police during the year. The major increases were in burglaries (394 compared to 295 in 1966), grand larcenies (241 in 1967, 163 in 1966), and assaults (191 against 151 the previous year). Crimes such as murder and rape, however, were rare; there were only two homicides (one was a traffic homicide) and three rapes in Kettering in 1967. Early in 1968 police pay was boosted again—the top patrolman's salary of $8,673 became one of the highest patrolman's pay scales in the state of Ohio and by far the best in the Dayton metropolitan area—and the force was increased in numbers to an authorized strength of fifty-three men. However, many officers maintained that any advantages that they might have gained in their fight against a rising crime rate through an increase in manpower were more than offset by U.S. Supreme Court rulings protecting suspects' rights against self-incrimination. Chief Shryock—while insisting that "police are to enforce whatever the laws are, whatever their interpretations are at the time"—said that the Court's 1966 Miranda decision created a situation in which police were "taking more reports of crimes and arresting fewer criminals." He speculated that "the hue and cry of communities will eventually cause the court to reweigh some of its ultraliberal interpretations."

Soon after the discovery of Barbara Ann Butler's body in the Ontario Store parking lot, Kettering police read to one Billy Joe Dean (a pseudonym) the rights against self-incrimination that the Miranda decision held he was entitled to:

"You have the right to remain silent.

"Anything you say can and will be used against you in a court of law.

"You have the right to a lawyer and have him present with you while you are being questioned.

"If you cannot afford to hire a lawyer, one will be appointed to represent you before any questioning if you wish one."

Dean, a good-looking nineteen-year-old with dark curly hair, was a prime suspect in the Butler murder because he had a record of a prior offense against a young woman in the Ontario Store parking lot.

On September 7, 1967, a Mary Elizabeth Sparks (a pseudonym) told Kettering police that a young man had attacked her in the Ontario Store parking lot with a knife and forced her to disrobe in her own car parked in the lot. Miss Sparks added that the assailant took $5.85 from her purse and that she escaped by leaping from her car, screaming, and running through the parking lot. From this and other information provided by the victim, Kettering police suspected that Dean, then eighteen and residing in the vicinity of the Ontario Store, was the assailant. Dean was picked up for questioning. He denied police accusations of his involvement in the attack upon Miss Sparks, claiming that he was on picket duty outside his employer's struck factory at the time of the incident. Police contacted the picket-line captain and were informed that Dean apparently had not picketed on September 7, 1967, because his name was not checked off for picket-duty pay on that date.

Having discredited Dean's alibi and having obtained a positive identification of Dean from the victim, police entered a formal charge of armed robbery against him on September 25, 1967. Dean pleaded not guilty to the charge and was released on his own recognizance. On November 22, 1967, the Montgomery County grand jury indicted Dean on the armed-robbery charge. Trial dates were set and reset. Finally, on March 18, 1968, Dean withdrew his plea of not guilty to the nonprobational offense of armed robbery and pleaded guilty "to the lesser and included offense of robbery." Robbery is a probational first offense in Ohio. Montgomery County Common Pleas Court Judge Cecil E. Edwards accepted Dean's guilty plea and referred his case to the county probation department for a recommendation as to Dean's fitness for probation. Dean was released on his own recognizance pending the judge's receipt of the probation department report, and the case was still awaiting final disposition when Barbara Butler was strangled to death on June 12.

Dean was picked up and questioned intensively about Miss Butler's death. He denied any involvement with the murder just as he had denied, at first, any connection with the 1967 attack on Mary Sparks. This time, however, Dean had an alibi. Police asked Dean—who worked from midnight to 8:00 A.M.—to state his whereabouts on the afternoon of Wednesday, June 12, and he answered, "Out riding around in my car." Dean had no witnesses to prove that he was just doing some innocent joy-riding at the time of Miss Butler's disappearance; police could find no witnesses to prove that he was not. The result was a Mexican standoff, with the police stuck with the burden of proof. Police needed evidence that would place Dean inside the death car before they could even think of placing a formal charge against him. They checked his finger and palm prints against the partial prints found in the Volkswagen; Dean's prints did not match with the partials. Police asked Dean to take a lie detector test; he agreed and passed the test. Police maintain that polygraph examinations are 99 percent accurate. The results of Dean's polygraph examination indicated that he was telling the truth when he said he did not kill Barbara Butler. Police could find nothing that would indicate that Dean knew or had ever met Miss Butler and they could think of no logical reason for his wanting to kill her. By stealing a small amount of money in the September, 1967, attack, Dean had "marked" himself as a thief; but Miss Butler's killer was apparently not a thief—nothing was missing from her purse or her auto. Also, there were indications that Dean had changed considerably since the 1967 crime— his job classification had improved from kitchen helper to assembler; his fifteen-year-old wife had given birth to a son; and the small family had moved from the neighborhood of the Ontario Store to a modern apartment in the city of Dayton.

Police thanked Dean for his cooperation and excused him from the case.

The removal of suspicion from Billy Joe Dean was the point at which the Butler murder became a mystery to the police. With Dean out, the police were left with no obvious suspect, several polyethylene bags full of evidence and some partial prints—all of which added up to nothing. The police sought evidence of a struggle at the apartments of the victim and her neighbors; they found none. The police scoured the area around the store in search of evidence that might pinpoint the place of her death—"nearly stripping," as a detective put it, "a self-service car-wash establishment down the road; we thought this was a likely place for an abductor to have taken the victim because he could have instant privacy just by pulling down the doors—but we found nothing." The police interviewed friends and acquaintances of the victim in hopes of finding a reason why one of these people might have wanted Barbara dead; they found no such motive but they did single out an ex-boyfriend "as someone to be set aside and thoroughly investigated." He was Kevin Drake (a pseudonym), a young high school teacher described to police as being "real odd."

The detective section of the Kettering Police Department numbered only eight men. Part of this tiny force was assigned to the task of "backgrounding" themselves on Kevin Drake prior to interviewing him and the remainder set to work checking out what Chief Shryock termed "many time-consuming leads received from the general public." The tips ranged from procedural suggestions from amateur detectives . . . to accusations of guilt made against personal enemies . . . to reported sightings of Miss Butler's Volkswagen after the time she was known to have left the store on June 12.

"In a case like this," Detective Lieutenant Albert Horn lamented, "some people will call you on anything. One man has called us seventeen times." The advice came by phone and by mail. Several letter writers suggested that the Kettering police solve the mystery with the help of "someone with extrasensory perception." One of these letters was written by an Indiana woman, who asked, "Why don't you call in a psychometrist? They can tell you a lot just by feeling an article that the victim has handled. . . . Good luck to you, and in case that you do, don't you think it would be worth something for this information I'm sending you? All I ask, KEEP MY NAME ABSOLUTELY MUM, even to your closest helpers and relatives please. P.S. Not even my hubby knows I'm writing to you on this. . . . KEEP MUM!" The Kettering police honored the woman's request for silence; they filed and forgot (for the time being) her letter and all others that suggested the use of extrasensory perception.

Other suggestions from the general public received more favorable response from the police. Police claimed that "a huge volume of tips were worked all the way out at a great deal of expense in time and money." One of these tips came from a minister who informed police that one of his parishioners had phoned him three nights after the murder to say, "I need help because the police are after me and I won't be taken alive." It took Kettering police several days to locate the man and learn that his fear of being "taken" by police stemmed from the fact that he had abandoned his wife and family after an argument and thought he was being sought for nonsupport.

A more promising lead came from a woman who told police she recalled seeing a silver-blue Volkswagen parked near a gravel pit outside Kettering's eastern boundary in Greene County on the afternoon of Barbara Butler's disappearance. Lieutenant Horn said later that "Sergeant Keith Thompson and I spent the better part of a day going all over that area around the gravel pit in hopes of finding something that would indicate it as the scene of the crime. We found nothing but, of course, we really didn't know what we were looking for other than maybe a blue terry cloth towel with a piece missing and the spool which the adhesive tape on the victim's arms came from."

On Monday, June 17, Kettering detectives attended Miss Butler's funeral. The officers indicated later that their attention was centered on one mourner above all others: a bearded young man named Kevin Drake. When Drake appeared at Kettering headquarters to be interviewed several days later he was beardless and had a story that police considered as clean-cut as his face. Drake said that he and Barbara Butler had a casual dating relationship extending from several months prior to her murder up to within a week and a half of it. He said that he was totally dedicated to his work and would "just go to Barbara's apartment to talk when I was done with my work." He said that he "sometimes didn't show up for dates until nine or eleven o'clock." Drake said that he came to feel that this arrangement was not fair to Miss Butler, so he told her, "I'm too busy to be tied down with one girl." Drake said that he learned that Miss Butler was missing on the evening of Wednesday, June 12, "when her roommate, Donna Gray, called me at my apartment to inquire if Barbara was with me." Miss Gray confirmed this part of Drake's story; so did a girl who said that she was visiting Drake at his apartment that evening. Drake said that he spent Thursday, June 13, "water skiing with a friend. I told my friend I was concerned about Barbara being missing," Drake added. The friend confirmed this and then said, "When we got back to Kettering that evening, I heard a report that a girl's body had been found in the Ontario parking lot. So I called police headquarters and asked, 'That girl they found: was her first name Barbara?' " Kettering police record all incoming phone calls on tape; the tape for June 13 was checked and the friend's voice was heard asking the question he said he had asked. Drake then "took and passed a lie-box test very well," Lieutenant Horn said. "Everything in Drake's story fit into place," the detective added.

The neighbor nurses—one of whom, Loretta Carmody, had found Miss Butler's body—were never formally suspected by Kettering police. Both girls were, however, extensively interviewed to the point that "Miss Carmody's parents got quite upset," Kettering Detective Sergeant Keith Thompson said. This was some time after Kettering officers attempted to make a discreet comparison of the tape found on the victim's arms with tape samples in the doctors' offices where the nurses were employed. "We waited until their next day off to do it," Lieutenant Horn said, "and asked the doctors not to mention what we were doing because we didn't want to upset the nurses. But when one of the nurses came to work the next day, the first thing her employer said to her was: 'Hey, the cops must think you killed your friend because they were in here yesterday checking our tape supply for evidence.' "

The doctor's loose tongue embarrassed the Kettering police; other mouths, however, were a source of far more serious police concern: they were a direct threat to the conduct of the investigation itself and they belonged to the many people who entered or looked into the Volkswagen after the discovery of the body. The police could ask that these people not tell their friends and acquaintances what they touched or saw inside the death car. But the police had to assume that these people were telling others such things as the color of the towel and blanket, what the handbag looked like, and where the packages were on the back seat. In an ideal police investigation the specific facts of the death scene would be known to only two parties: the police and the killer. Under ideal conditions, specific facts are more than evidence—they are tools which the police can use as controls in the evaluation of statements and the discrediting of false confessions. For example, a specific fact of the Butler case was that the color of the towel atop the body was yellow. An excellent question to put to a subject undergoing polygraph examination would have been: What was the color of the towel? The subject's answer and measured reaction would have been highly informative to police if they could have been certain that the color of the towel was known to only themselves and the killer. But the Kettering police had to assume that the color of the towel and many other specific facts of the death scene were widely known and thus relatively worthless as investigative tools. Lieutenant Al Horn told me later, "The investigation would have been a good deal smoother, and we could have been a lot freer with you newspaper guys, if we didn't have to worry about so many people knowing so damn much."

The police search for Barbara Butler's killer was concentrated on the Greater Dayton area although a nationwide teletype advisory sought information on similar crimes on the chance that the murderer was an itinerant. Replies to the advisory failed to turn up another crime that matched the Butler murder in all of its bizarre aspects. Kettering Police Chief Shryock took the position that "our killer could be anybody—that's one of the reasons why this crime is so unusual." Having no firm suspicions about any one individual, the police had loose suspicions about everybody—myself, I am sure, included. One day a detective prefaced his answer to a question by warning me: "You already know so many facts of this case that I couldn't discredit your confession if you were to tell me that you killed Barbara Butler." Another time a detective suggested to me, "Let's have a cup of coffee." When I accepted the offer, he insisted on preparing it himself. He went to the outer office of the detective section and returned carrying a china mug full of hot coffee in a most unusual manner: with only the thumb and forefinger of his right hand touching the sides of the mug. I assumed that the man wanted my fingerprints on the handle of the mug so I obliged him in as ostentatious a manner as I could manage.

While the investigation was in one of its most intense periods, Chief Shryock's attention was distracted by a "Summer in the City" group of activists from Dayton, who appeared in Kettering to picket and hand out leaflets in protest of alleged "shoot to wound" orders issued Kettering police in the event the all-white suburb should be invaded by outsiders bent on racial violence. The title of the leaflets was "Hysteria Hits Kettering." The leaflets did not mention the Butler case. However, if there was hysteria in Kettering at the time, it was due to the finding of a girl's body in a parking lot, not to a fear of racial disturbance.

People talked about the murder and worried about the possibility of the killer striking again. Women went furtively in and out of stores in the area. Two sheriff's detectives began moonlighting the sale of pocketbook tear gas canisters, one of them telling me, "You better get one of these for your wife if she goes to the store by herself very often."

I visited the Ontario Store parking lot several times in the weeks following the murder and noted that the parking space where the death car had been found was vacant even during peak business hours when all of the other parking spaces around it were occupied.

The parking space where the car and body had been discovered was easily recognizable because its black asphalt surface was smeared with a large splotch of dried white paint. The paint had been spilled on the parking space sometime before the murder. But police did not know this when they arrived on the Ontario Store lot on the afternoon of Thursday, June 13.

Shortly after the discovery of the body a policeman noted "a white smear" on the parking lot pavement beneath the Volkswagen. Police felt, at the time, that the "white smear" might have some relationship to the presence of the body in the Volkswagen and they decided to move the car in order to examine the spot on the pavement. In the process the police unintentionally added a classic note of irony to the case: they picked up the Volkswagen and carried it to an adjoining parking space—doing the very thing to the murdered girl's car that her friends said had upset her so in life!

Prior to 1968 Kettering police could boast of a record of no unsolved homicides. Now the small suburban department was charged with solving a murder that might have confounded detectives on the largest and best equipped police force in the world. Without leaving a clue to his identity, a phantom had apparently abducted a "nice girl who didn't have an enemy in the world" from a busy parking lot in broad daylight for the sole purpose of strangling her to death. Detective Sergeant Jim Tobias said the Butler case had this impact on his life and feelings: "I've looked down the barrels of a shotgun in the hands of a guy who had good reason to kill me . . . taken the shotgun away . . . gone home and had a couple of beers. But this case: I wake up in the middle of the night and the first thing I think of is Barbara Butler . . . who killed Barbara Butler?"

The murder was so senseless that police began to wonder if the killer might realize this himself in a moment of clarity, begin to brood over what he had done, and commit suicide as proof of his sorrow. The Kettering police made inquiries on all unexplained deaths in the Dayton area and three late-June suicides attracted their very close attention.

The first of these occurred a week after Miss Butler's death, in the contiguous suburb of Moraine. The police investigation indicated that a young man had killed himself for no apparent reason. "The timing was good as a possible link to the Butler case," a detective said, "but further checks revealed that the man was involved in an automobile accident fifty miles away at the time Miss Butler was leaving the store."

The second suicide was perhaps the most interesting. On Saturday, June 29—seventeen days after the murder—the partially clad body of a fifty-one-year-old salesman was discovered by his estranged wife on the bathroom floor of a Woodman Park Drive apartment located only a hundred paces from the front door of the apartment formerly occupied by Barbara Butler. There were no signs of violence on the body, but a recently fired pistol was found on a bed in a room adjacent to the bathroom and there was a bullet hole in the frame of a wall mirror directly across the room from the bed. The man was identified as Martin Carl Ernst (a pseudonym). A postmortem examination determined that he had died of a self-administered overdose of barbiturates. Investigators wondered: Was Ernst aiming at his own image—an image he hated because of some dreadful thing he had done—when he fired the shot at the mirror? When police learned that Ernst had not moved into his apartment until several days after Miss Butler's death and that he was a hundred miles from Kettering, in Indianapolis, on the day of the murder, they decided that Ernst's suicide had no possible connection with the Butler case. That was a police decision; others were not so sure. A coroner's investigator said he learned that Ernst "was the kind of guy who fell in love all over the place. His wife left him because he was constantly going after one woman after another . . . and the younger they were the better he liked them."

The third suicide victim was, according to Greene County Sheriff Russ Bradley, "the most likely dead suspect the Kettering police had in the Butler case." On Saturday, July 13, "the badly decomposed body of a twenty-year-old man, later identified as Kent Miles [a pseudonym], was found hanging from a tree in a wooded area near a church," according to an investigator's report. The death scene was only a few miles from Kettering in Greene County (the city's eastern boundary is also the dividing line between Montgomery and Greene counties). It was estimated that the young man had been dead two to three weeks. His earliest time of death was June 22, or ten days after the murder—which is, a detective said, "About the length of time it takes some of these kooks to go through the grieving bit and make up their minds to kill themselves."

Miles's finger and palm prints were not on file and his corpse was too badly decomposed to permit the taking of print specimens. Police were thus unable to "place" Miles inside the Volkswagen through comparison with the partial prints found in the death car. However, a Kettering detective thought, "We could have built a pretty good circumstantial case against Miles. He was almost a neighbor of Butler's at the Woodman Park apartments. He was in her age group and apparently did a lot of socializing. We can't establish his whereabouts on the day of the murder. Something was wrong with him or he wouldn't have killed himself. But you can't try a dead man, so we can't prove that Miles was the killer."

To Kettering Chief Shryock's credit, he did not do what many police officers might have done under similar circumstances; he did not just close the case and begin to say privately that he "knew" but could not prove who the killer was. Chief Shryock said that the Butler case would remain open. "We're not going to put this thing in a file marked done," he insisted. "Many things are still being worked on."

9

In July the situation deteriorated from bad to worse to almost comical.

Two evidence-analysis reports were received by Kettering police during the month and both of them were negative. On July 7 the coroner reported that analysis of acid extractions had determined that Miss Butler's system contained no incapacitating drugs "for which there is a known test." Coroner's Chief Investigator Harry Bloomer said that the acid extraction work had been done by a private chemist on a contract basis. "It took him nearly a month to complete the report," Bloomer lamented, "even though we asked that it be done on a rush basis." Other tests had indicated earlier that drugs were not a factor in Miss Butler's death, but the acid extraction results made matters final: the police now had no hope of obtaining a medical explanation of why the victim did not struggle with her killer. A few days later police received even more depressing news from Washington. Federal Bureau of Investigation laboratory experts reported that they had analyzed the Butler case evidence and had come to the conclusion that it was "foreign to us." This meant that the partial finger and palm prints, the brown string, the clothing of the victim, the tape, the swatch of blue terry cloth, and all other items found in the death car bore no clues to the killer's identity. The FBI was also unable to detect any flesh particles in the items submitted to it for examination—leaving the police still uncertain as to what the murder weapon was and completely at a loss to explain how the unknown weapon had been used to cause strangulation without leaving marks all the way around the neck.

Next there occurred an incident that could have happened only in a nation where the process of justice is slow and balanced in favor of the accused and in an area of that nation where the channels of communication between neighboring law-enforcement agencies are poor.

The strange story of Bobby D. Neal's (a pseudonym) involvement in the Butler case began in Greene County on February 14, 1968. On that date Neal was arrested by Greene County officers and charged with rape. Neal, a twenty-year-old college student, pleaded guilty to a reduced charge of assault and battery. He was free on bond and awaiting sentencing when, on June 1, 1968, he was arrested in the Greene County city of Fairborn and charged with assault with intent to rape another girl. He pleaded not guilty to this charge and was released on five hundred dollars bond.

On July 1, 1968, the partially clothed body of a Mrs. Patricia H. Burns (a pseudonym), a thirty-year-old factory worker and the mother of two minor children, was found in her Fairborn home. Fairborn police said, "An aura of mystery surrounds Mrs. Burns's death. She was a young woman in apparent good health. But there were no indications of violence, force, or resistance on her body or in her home." An autopsy was ordered.

Greene County Prosecutor Marshall E. Peterson began to think about Bobby D. Neal. "His assaults—the one he was convicted of and the one he was awaiting prosecution for—were not in the classic sense," Peterson said. "There was no tearing of clothing or anything like that."

Greene County Coroner Dr. J. G. Krause detected sperm in Mrs. Burns's mouth during the course of a postmortem examination and ruled her death "a possible homicide due to reasons obscure." He also said, "We are thinking of the possibility of a connection between Mrs. Burns's death and the Butler case in Kettering."

The "possible connection" was Bobby D. Neal. Kettering police were informed of the conviction, charge, and suspicion that Neal was under in neighboring Greene County. They also learned that Neal was a motorcycle enthusiast who commuted daily from his home in Greene County to the campus of Wright State University—which is adjacent to both the school where Miss Butler taught and the apartment complex where she resided.

On the morning of Monday, July 8, Kettering police began making what Chief Shryock termed "an inquiry about Neal." Detectives thought that the fact that Neal rode a motorcycle fit in with the theory that Barbara Butler had been abducted from the Ontario Store lot in her own car. "If Neal was the killer," a detective reasoned, "he would have had to take her away in her own car 'cause he couldn't have put her on that little Honda of his." Alas, when the detective was speaking those words both Bobby D. Neal and his Honda motorcycle were no more.

At noon of the very day that Kettering police learned of Neal, his motorcycle skidded on wet pavement and struck an automobile. Neal was dead on arrival at a Dayton hospital a half hour later. Chief Shryock said Neal's death was "a real tragedy for us. We thought we had something because his MO in the Greene County assaults was not brutal and a lot like the Butler case. He warranted a real checking out even though his prints would not match with the partials found in the Volkswagen."

Greene County Prosecutor Marshall Peterson termed the young man's death "the strangest thing that ever happened to me. About one o'clock on that Monday, I was in the judge's chambers talking with the judge and Neal's attorney. We were waiting for Neal, who was due in court at that time for a pretrial conference on the assault-with-intent-to-rape charge. My secretary called me from the judge's chambers to tell me there was no use in our waiting for Neal—he had died en route to court."

On the evening of Monday, July 8, the Dayton *Daily News* printed a caricature of Chief Shryock alongside editorial page criticism of his department's conduct of the Butler investigation. The cartoon depicted the chief, dressed in Sherlock Holmes attire, walking in circles about numerous items of evidence and mumbling, "A clue, a clue, if only I had a clue."

The editorial comment was based on a July 5 statement by Montgomery County Prosecutor Lee C. Falke. On that date, Falke had proposed that "special crimes such as the Butler case be handled by a metropolitan squad of police experts." Falke said the Kettering police "are doing the best job they can with the number of personnel they have available, but we ought to have had the best men from all our law-enforcement agencies working on the Butler case. . . . Because of recent Supreme Court decisions, scientific police work is needed more than it ever was."

The editorial endorsed the prosecutor's proposal and then alleged: "It tells no secrets out of school to point out that the Kettering police have floundered on this case. . . . The simple fact is that not one police department in the Dayton metropolitan area, except the one in the City of Dayton, is anywhere near equipped and manned to deal with murders. You can repeat that for virtually every large metropolitan area in the nation. As a nation, we are the victims of thousands of police departments in tiny jurisdictions, unable to operate well across municipal lines, budget-starved, inadequately manned and not possessed of much in the way of sophisticated equipment."

On Tuesday, July 9, Chief Shryock announced to the press that all future Kettering police statements on the Butler case would be made personally, by him. However, the weekly Kettering-Oakwood *Times* was already in possession of a statement on the Butler case from Kettering Police Lieutenant Albert Horn; the statement was printed on Thursday, July 11, under the headline: "CITY POLICE WOULD WELCOME SERVICES OF A CLAIRVOYANT." In the body of the story, Lieutenant Horn was quoted as saying that Kettering police were "up against a wall" in the Butler investigation and "would cooperate in any possible way should persons with psychic powers offer their services to help solve this most baffling crime."

I read those words and began to snicker. I thought: What next? I pointed out the story to police reporter Denny Gilbert and said, "Can you imagine those Kettering cops being so confused over the murder that they are willing to listen to the babblings of a fortuneteller? Can't you just picture a couple of detectives sneaking about the countryside—with hat brims pulled down and coat collars turned up—as a swami in pointed hat and long robes shows them the way? It's ridiculous!"

"It might not be as crazy as you think," Gilbert replied. "I was talking to a couple of Dayton dicks this morning and they claim that there's a medium here in town who told them that she knows all about the murder of the girl in the Volkswagen."

"You can't be serious!"

"Those two Dayton detectives were very serious. They've got a fugitive warrant for some guy who has an aunt by the name of Mrs. Beatrice Cook [a pseudonym]. The detectives went to see the aunt. This Mrs. Cook tells the cops that she's a medium. Then, they say, she proved it to them by telling them a lot of obscure information about themselves and their families."

"What did she tell them?"

"I don't know all the details, but one detective says she told him the name of his wife's uncle. He was very impressed because he'd forgotten the uncle's name and had to call up his wife to find out that Mrs. Cook was right."

"What did this Mrs. Cook tell the detectives about the fugitive?"

"That I don't know—but I'm gonna go see this Mrs. Cook and find out what she knows about the Butler case."

"I'll go with you—I can use a good laugh!"

Mrs. Beatrice Cook welcomed us into her small frame home on Dayton's east side with the word that "the spirit told me to expect you two reporters." Biting our lips to keep from laughing, we listened as the elderly little woman explained: "I'm a spiritualist. I talk to the spirit. I learned how from my mother who came over from Ireland. The spirit tells me everything."

I asked, "Has the spirit given you any hints about who killed Barbara Butler?"

"Certainly," she replied. Then she launched into a long-winded tale about two schoolteachers who had visited her several weeks before the murder to have their fortunes told. This is the gist of Mrs. Cook's story:

"One schoolteacher had her hair piled up on her head, fancy-like, so I told her she'd got rid of two husbands—by divorce, that is—and, sure enough, she had. I told the other one I saw the name Barbara in her reading . . . and she says, 'You must mean Barbara Butler.' I told her I didn't know the last name but I saw a Barbara lying on the front floor of a car. I thought, then, that she'd been in an accident . . . but, after I heard she was killed, I knew she was strangled. I see that blanket tucked all around the body and the towel around her neck. Do you want to know who killed her?"

"Who?" Gilbert and I asked in one voice.

Mrs. Cook glanced about her living room in the manner of a back-fence gossip about to unload a juicy item on a neighbor. Then, in a voice that was almost a whisper, she said, "I can't say the killer's name to you, but I can spell it. First name: A-L-L-A-N. Last name: B-A-R-G-U-E-N."

Mrs. Cook explained: "The spirit doesn't pronounce names of people to me—he just tells me the letters of their names."

I pronounced the name as "Bar-go-en."

Mrs. Cook insisted, "I don't know the pronunciation. But I did have a vision about this B-A-R-G-U-E-N fella. I saw him meeting Barbara Butler in the store parking lot . . . she went off with him in his Chevrolet car . . . they went to a

67

motel or a restaurant and ate something . . . he killed her after that as she was standing by her car . . . he was gonna throw her body in the river, but he didn't . . . he works at NCR . . . he's a computer expert and she was going to be working with him on her new job . . . he drives a car with a yellow-colored license plate—a Connecticut license plate."

I told Mrs. Cook that I believed that Connecticut license plates were blue and white. She allowed, "Maybe I'm off on the state . . . but the rest of what I told you is right. . . . You'll find out that's so when you check up on this man B-A-R-G-U-E-N."

"Mrs. Cook," I asked, "you said you could see the color of the license plate. . . . Your visions are in color, then?"

"Yes."

"Then, Mrs. Cook, what was the color of the towel you saw in the vision?"

"Er . . . bluish-green?"

We said good-by to Mrs. Cook. The color of the towel, of course, was yellow. The color had never been printed in a newspaper article but was rather common knowledge as a result of so many people having seen it in the Volkswagen after the discovery of the body. However, that bit of common knowledge hadn't yet reached Mrs. Cook, or her spirit friend.

I was certain that Mrs. Beatrice Cook was a phony. Nevertheless, I wondered where she had come up with the name Allan Barguen. Officials at the National Cash Register Company had never heard of such a person and the name Barguen was not listed in any Dayton directories. Then I pronounced B-A-R-G-U-E-N several times as "bar-go-en" and realized where Mrs. Cook had come up with that name: right out of a quote in one of the newspaper stories I had written on the case—Kettering Detective Sergeant Jim Tobias commenting that Barbara Butler "definitely was not the *bar-going* type."

10

In late July the situation appeared hopeless. All of the live suspects had been checked out and set aside. Four dead suspects were beyond the reach of any earthly investigation. The volume of leads and tips coming in to the police had thinned down to a trickle. Investigators had gone down one dead-end trail after another. The evidence of the case proved only one thing: that a girl had been murdered.

I had come to a point where I was more inclined to laugh at police actions and statements than I was to sympathize with their plight. I was discouraged and tired because almost all of my efforts on the case in recent weeks had been fruitless and had been done on my own time after the completion of regular assignments.

So on July 21 I wrote a wrap-up story, thinking that the words in the article would be the last I would ever write on the murder of Barbara Butler. Then I filed away seven notebooks of quotes and information on the case and made a determined effort to work my regular newspaper assignments with an enthusiasm that had been lacking during the many weeks when my prime interest in life had been one of seeking answers to questions posed by a mysterious death.

"It's all over," I told my wife. "I'm not going to have anything more to do with that damned murder case. Call up some of your friends and tell them we're still in town and ready to play bridge any night they can come over." That statement will never wind up in an anthology of famous last words—unless my wife decides to publish a collection of them someday. The truth was that I was not finished with the murder case—I was on the eve of getting really involved in it. Up until this point my association with the murder investigation had been that of an interested spectator—a newspaper reporter who asked questions and wrote stories based on information given him by other people. The events of the next few weeks caused a radical change in my status. Kettering Lieutenant Horn said that the change meant: "I'll have to put you in the casebook now—you've become a part of the investigation."

In the last week of July three things happened that, at the time, seemed to be completely unrelated incidents—to each other and to the murder case.

First, a neighbor of ours told my wife that she had dated Kevin Drake—the high school teacher who had been interviewed by the police early in the case—several times before he began to date Barbara Butler. She said, among other things, that Drake was a physical-culture enthusiast who had exercise equipment in his apartment and was very particular about the food he ate and the manner in which it was prepared.

Secondly, I wrote a humorous feature story on another topic that drew a critical unsigned letter from a reader. There was no venom in the letter; it merely contained an implication that I should get back to the serious business of solving a murder and quit wasting time writing funny stories. The letter was handwritten and the person who wrote it did not connect the letter *y* with the letter following it; for example, Dayton was written *Day ton*. I sensed that there was something strange about the letter and I kept it.

Thirdly, Mrs. Linda Keagan (a pseudonym), an old friend of my wife's with whom we had resumed a relationship during July—she visited our apartment several times, talking over many matters, including the murder case and my work on it—phoned our home and, after conversing with Charlotte for several minutes, asked to speak to me. She began talking at great length about Kevin Drake. Mrs. Keagan, a young widow who had resumed a teaching career following the death of her husband the year before, said that she and Drake had recently been among a group of chaperons who accompanied some Dayton schoolchildren on a summer outing to a zoo. Linda Keagan said she thought I ought to know that Drake "has been acting very strange lately. His friends think it has something to do with the murder." She described Drake as being "a big strong guy with a very weak stomach." She said she knew about his intestinal weakness because: "When we took the kids to the zoo, the smells made Drake so sick he had to leave the tour group and wait for us outside in the bus."

Mrs. Keagan's remarks were interesting, I thought, and somewhat incriminatory of Kevin Drake when I recalled police speculation that Miss Butler's killer may not have gone through with the sex act because his passions may have cooled when he discovered that she was in her menstrual cycle. Drake, according to Mrs. Keagan, was a big strong guy with a weak stomach. If zoo smells upset Drake, I wondered, what would the sight of menstrual blood have done to him?

I had no reason to question the accuracy of Mrs. Keagan's statements about Drake or the reason for her making them to me. As far as I knew, Linda Keagan had no more interest in the murder, or its solution, than the average Daytonian. She was, I believed, merely attempting to help out a reporter friend working on the case by passing along information concerning Drake—a person she was aware (either from what we had told her or she had learned through the school-system grapevine) had had a dating relationship with the victim.

Later my wife was to remind me that "Linda tends to exaggerate a lot." She added, "She can't stand to talk about her husband's death. But after he died [of cancer in his mid-twenties] that's all her friends could think of to talk to her about. So she blows up everyday things into big deals to change the subject or get people to listen to her. She's a very social-minded person who needs to be with people and have them notice her."

As nearly as Dale Huffman could recall, the phone call was made "about ten-thirty" on the morning of Monday, July 29. Huffman, a *Daily News* police reporter, was on duty in the press room of the Dayton Safety Building at the time. The phone rang, he answered it, and the search for Barbara Butler's killer turned into a strange game of mental tag in which I was It!

Huffman reconstructed the phone call, which, he said, "was from a very soft-spoken woman," this way:

"In the early part of the conversation, the woman pounded on one thing: she kept saying she had to be certain that I was not a police officer. I finally got her convinced that I was a newspaper reporter. Then she asked if I covered stories in the Kettering area. I said I did and told her my name two or three times. There were a lot of pauses. Then she asked, 'Do you cover murders?' I didn't get a chance to answer because she followed up her question by telling me, 'I know something about a murder, but I don't know how to

71

say it or who to tell it to. I don't want to say it to a cop. If I tell you what I want to tell you, I hope it won't be used against me.' I asked her name and what murder she was talking about. She wouldn't tell me her name; she just answered: 'I think I know something about the Barbara Butler case that should be known. It's been bothering me so much that I can't sleep at night.'

"With that I got real interested. I asked the woman what she knew. But she just kept repeating stuff like, 'You're a cop . . . the cops are recording this call.' I think she was scared 'cause she could hear police calls on the loudspeaker. I tried to turn down the volume, but I couldn't reach the switch. Any other time of day, there would have been half a dozen Dayton detectives in and out of the press room during the time I was on the phone with that woman; but not one came in when I really needed him to put a trace on the call. I was afraid that the woman was going to hang up on me so I suggested, 'May I meet you somewhere to allay your fears that this call is being recorded?'

"She asked, 'Will you meet me on my own grounds?' I said, 'Yes! Where?' We just started to arrange a meeting place when she said, 'Somebody is coming into the office . . . I have to hang up.' There was a click on the line."

Huffman advised the city desk of the mysterious phone call and a *Daily News* line was kept open the rest of the day in hopes that the woman would call back; she did not.

What did the call mean? I would have considered it the work of a crank if the call had been made a few days after the murder or at a time when the case was getting a great deal of publicity. But it seemed "too late in the day" for a crank—the murder investigation was in its seventh week and not a word had been printed or broadcast on the case in over a week. I also would have thought that the call was from a crank if the caller had begun the conversation by proclaiming: "I know who killed Barbara Butler!" But the woman had made no such grand announcement—Huffman indicated that he almost had to coax the name Barbara Butler out of the woman. I thus considered the call to be genuine and an indication that something was stirring beneath the surface of a murder case that had appeared dormant for some time.

The phone call from the woman who "knew something" triggered these actions and reactions:

Jim Fain, editor of the Dayton *Daily News,* was informed

of the phone call. Fain asked me to tell him everything that I knew about Barbara Butler's murder. I told him. Fain said he was "fascinated" and wanted to know more, even if the information was such that it could not be used in a newspaper story. I was assigned to the case full-time and told "don't worry about writing a story, just find out everything you can about the murder even if it means going back over a lot of ground that the police have already covered."

When the boss said "everything" he meant, of course, the very thing that nobody had been able to find out: Who killed Barbara Butler?

On Tuesday, July 30, I went to Kettering and told Chief John Shryock of the phone call and my assignment to the case on a full-time, no-story basis. The chief said that he thought the phone call "could be an indication that somebody's conscience is bothering them. . . . We certainly hope so." He also said he appreciated my newspaper's "continuing interest" in the Butler case.

"How can I help?" I asked. "Is there anybody that I can question as a newspaperman: someone you would like to question, but can't, because of Supreme Court limitations on what you can ask a suspect without a lawyer present?" Shryock never answered me, but he did have a suggestion:

"Talk to Lieutenant Al Horn when he gets back in town on Thursday. He may know of an area of this case in which you can be of some help to us."

I spent the rest of Tuesday and all of Wednesday, July 31, doing two things. At the suggestion of the police I wrote a synopsis, five thousand words in length, of the case as I knew it at the time. (Two Kettering detectives read the report and then told me it was "accurate except for maybe a couple of things." When I asked permission to read the police casebook in order to become 100 percent accurate on the facts of the case, Keith Thompson, who had recently been promoted from sergeant to lieutenant in the Kettering department, replied, "We're not going to let you see our casebook!")

I also talked to various lawyers on the theory that the woman with the troubled conscience might have sought legal advice. I found no lawyer who would admit to having such a client. I decided that if a troubled conscience had moved the woman to telephone, her conscience would have been eased by the very act of making the call and it now might take several weeks before her conscience would start bothering her again. So on Thursday, August 1, I dropped the subject and called on Lieutenant Horn to see what he had in mind for me. Horn's "area of help" was, as I might have guessed, extrasensory perception. I told the lieutenant of my experience with Mrs. Beatrice Cook. "I've got better things to do than waste my time talking to fortunetellers," I insisted.

"Now, now," Horn said, "maybe you got onto a bad apple the first time around. I'll admit that I'm skeptical of this ESP stuff myself. But a lot of police departments around the world are using clairvoyants on difficult cases. Here," he said, taking a letter out of a manila folder and handing it to me, "take a look at this."

The letter was dated June 19 (one week after the murder) and was addressed to the Kettering Police Department. In part, it said:

With regard to the recent murder . . . has your agency considered utilizing the services of a clairvoyant?

Although there is skepticism in some quarters relative to such persons' psychic powers, Holland, as well as Great Britain, frequently engages paragnosts in attempting to solve perplexing crimes.

One of the outstanding clairvoyants, Gerald Croiset, in close association with Professor Tenhaeff, of the University of Utrecht, Netherlands, has been called upon in several instances to aid in breaking some of America's toughest cases. This he has done . . . merely by having sent to him some item (inductor) associated with the deceased and/or crime. One in particular was the case of four-year-old Edith (Google) Kiecorius of Brooklyn . . . in 1961. In that instance . . . Croiset was able to conjure up mental images of the locale, descriptions of the involved premises —as well as that of the suspect, even before any items had been sent to him. . . .

Surely, if all other avenues fail it would be worth a try to consult a recognized clairvoyant, for as I'm sure you have heard, they do not seek remuneration, feeling that were they to do so they would be deprived of this innate gift.

Understandably, consulting a psychic might "go against the grain" of those trained to pursue a more logical course. However, I'm confident this suggestion will be shown the same consideration as those received from other concerned and interested citizens.

The typewritten letter was signed by a Mrs. William (Alice) Seckinger (a pseudonym) of Kettering, Ohio. A notation on the top of the letter indicated that it had been received by Kettering police on June 21, 1968, at 9:30 A.M.

Lieutenant Horn asked me what I thought of the letter. I answered him by saying, "The woman expresses herself well. She doesn't sound like a kook."

"Why don't you take this letter and go see the woman," Horn suggested. "Maybe she can tell you the names of some recognized clairvoyants in this area."

"Lieutenant, if you believe that a clairvoyant can help solve the murder, why don't you go see the woman yourself?"

"We look at this woman's suggestion as an opportunity to do a little experimenting in modern police methods. If I were to work directly with a clairvoyant and the experiment didn't work out, it might leave the department open to ridicule."

"Are you saying you want me to be a go-between?"

"I wouldn't put it in those words. You might get yourself quite a story if you find a clairvoyant who is able to help us solve the case. If you agree to help us, this is the way we'll do it: you will talk to a clairvoyant, write down everything that he says, bring the information to me, and I will be the judge of its content."

"May I ask how you intend to do that?"

"We've got to be very cautious."

"I would say that you have already proved that point . . . the woman wrote that letter six weeks ago."

"We couldn't even consider using an unproved approach like ESP until after all accepted investigative procedures had failed. We don't really expect much now. We just want you to talk to a clairvoyant and see what he's got to say. If he should come up with something that we know to be a fact of the case—a fact that he couldn't have learned from reading the newspapers—then we would give serious consideration to things that he might tell us about the case of which we have no certain knowledge."

"Okay. A clairvoyant tells me that the color of the towel in the death car is yellow, then he names a particular individual as Barbara Butler's murderer. . . . Would you believe it?"

"No! I wouldn't begin to accept a clairvoyant's information unless he had hit on something much more obscure than the color of the towel. . . . He would have to tell me a fact of this case that you are not even aware of yourself."

The lieutenant had hit me in a vulnerable spot: my curiosity to know all that there was to know about the murder. I knew that I had to cooperate with the police in order to have any hope of satisfying my curiosity. I told the lieutenant that I would call on Mrs. Seckinger. I walked out the door of the Kettering police station about three o'clock in the afternoon of Thursday, August 1, 1968, and headed into the most fascinating and frightening experience of my life.

11

The nameplate on the door identified the occupant of the apartment as: "Seckinger, Mrs. Wm." I knocked. In response, the door opened about three inches until it caught on a chain lock. In the space between the door and the doorframe I saw part of a woman's face. The woman asked my business. I handed the letter through the aperture and asked, "Did you write this, ma'am?"

The woman took the letter, scanned it for a moment, and then replied, "Yes, I believe I did. I'm Alice Seckinger. Are you from the police?" I told Mrs. Seckinger who I was and why I was there. She undid the chain lock, opened the door, and welcomed me into her apartment.

In full view, Mrs. Alice Seckinger was tall, slender, and quite attractive. I guessed her age to be middle-to-late forties. Her hair, liberally streaked with gray, was neatly done. She was wearing a light-colored suit, high heels, nylons, and a considerable amount of makeup. I looked at my wristwatch: 3:30 P.M. We exchanged pleasantries. I sat down on an expensive-looking white couch and let my eyes roam about Mrs. Seckinger's well-furnished living room. Everything was immaculate.

I wondered: What is this? What have I walked into? Not many women get all dressed up in the middle of the afternoon just to sit around a spick-and-span apartment. Could she have been expecting me? No! She couldn't have known I was coming because I didn't know it myself until a half hour ago.

The woman said, "I want to explain about the chain lock. I only started using it during the day after what happened to that girl in the parking lot."

"A woman who lives by herself can't be too careful these days," I said, hoping to learn something from her response.

"Yes!"

"Mrs. Seckinger, is this a bad time for you? I mean, I didn't interrupt anything, did I?"

"Oh, no. Why do you ask?"

"I thought perhaps you might be going out or expecting someone."

"No."

"Well, then, you know I'm here because of your suggestion to the Kettering police. Do you know of any clairvoyants in the Dayton area who might be willing to help on the murder case?"

"I know of two persons who would probably welcome an opportunity to try and help. The first is very well known in those circles under her maiden name of Hester Jones. Her married name is Mrs. Grant [a pseudonym]."

"Those circles?" I asked. "What do you mean by that?"

"People with an interest in extrasensory perception."

"I suppose there are quite a few people in this area with such an interest."

"Yes! One of the spiritualist churches in town has quite an active group."

"I'll bet. What was the second name you were going to give me?"

"Norman Dodd [a pseudonym]—he's just a young fellow but he apparently has quite a gift."

"Why do you say that?"

"Because he told me some things that later turned out to be true."

"What things?"

"Oh, it's a long story that I'd rather not get into."

"May I ask what you know about this fellow Dodd?"

"Well, I would say that he's in his middle-to-late twenties. He told me that he first became aware of his clairvoyant abilities last Christmas. He came downstairs Christmas morning, looked at the wrapped packages under the tree, and told his wife what each package contained."

"Without opening the packages?"

"Yes. He was very frightened by the experience."

77

"Hmmm. Well, you've told me that Dodd is married. Does he have any children?"

"I believe so; two girls and a boy, I think."

"Anything else about him?"

"No, I don't believe so."

"Where can I get in contact with these people—Mrs. Grant and Mr. Dodd?" I asked.

"Well, you can reach Mrs. Grant at her home anytime. But you would have to wait until evening if you want to talk to Norman Dodd—he works in a factory daytimes and never gets home until after five."

Mrs. Seckinger gave me the addresses and phone numbers of the two alleged clairvoyants. I thanked her for her assistance and left the apartment. I went to the Dayton *Daily News* building and told my managing editor, Greg Favre, what the Kettering police had asked of me and what I was doing about it. Favre's reaction was: "It won't hurt to see what these so-called clairvoyants have got to say. I'd do it by phone, though. That way you can always hang up if they start spouting a lot of nonsense that has nothing to do with the murder."

I agreed. I also told my boss that I was extremely wary of the whole business. "I've got a feeling that Mrs. Seckinger wants me to call Dodd second—if at all. So I'm going to go at it the other way around; I'm going to wait until after five o'clock and call Dodd first."

About 5:45 P.M., on Thursday, August 1, I dialed Norman Dodd's telephone number from my desk at the *Daily News*.

A woman's voice said, "Hello."

"May I speak to Norman Dodd, please?"

"Just a moment."

I heard a sound that indicated to me that the phone had been put down on a table. I heard a background yell of "Honey, it's for you."

A moment later a deliberate, medium-pitched male voice said, "This is Norman Dodd."

"Hello. I'm Bill Clark, a reporter at the *Daily News*. . . . A Mrs. Alice Seckinger suggested that I call."

"Mrs. Who? What name did you say?"

"Seckinger . . . Mrs. Alice Seckinger."

"I'm afraid I don't know anybody by that name."

"You must—she gave me your name and telephone number."

"Oh, perhaps she is the woman I helped find the rapist

78

for . . . yes, that must be it. Her daughter was raped and I described a man to her that I had never seen before. . . . He turned out to be the criminal."

I thought: Some clairvoyant this guy must be—he doesn't even know the name of a woman he claims to have found a rapist for.

Just to see what Dodd would say next, I asked, "You say you caught a rapist—does that mean you are a clairvoyant? Is that what I should call you?"

"Many do," he replied matter-of-factly, "those I have helped, that is. . . . Oh, and there have been so many that I have helped, I can't always remember their names . . . names mean nothing to me, you see. May I help you?"

"Well, I called to inquire if you might be able to get something on a murder case I've been working on."

Dodd laughed and then said, "A murder? I've never done anything on a matter quite so serious . . . but I recently helped to locate two missing children. Took the parents to within two blocks of where the children were eventually found in New York City."

I wondered what Dodd took me for—if he had found any missing children I would have known about it because we would have splashed a story like that all over our front page.

"You found some missing kids, eh," I said. "Did we have a story on that in the *Daily News?*"

"I do not permit my efforts to be publicized," Dodd snapped; "it is one of the things that I insist upon before I attempt to help people. I do not subscribe to any newspapers and never read them because it might confuse me—muddle up my mind with meaningless details—if I should read about something I am later asked to give assistance on. I do not know if I can help you with this murder, but I will try if you will guarantee that there will be no publicity and no money."

I told him that the no-payment stipulation was an easy condition, but I added, "We'll have to write something if you solve the murder. We could probably do it without using your name if you insist."

Dodd changed the subject: "My degree of efficiency is not something I can turn on and off. I don't know when or how I can help you . . . but I have recently been in a period of rest. I told my wife last night that the rest period is about to end—there is something I am going to be asked to do that is important."

"Well, this is a very important murder case. A girl was strangled in Kettering nearly two months ago and the police—"

"Wait!" Dodd interrupted. "Say no more—I'm getting something! You must be a sender! You said, 'girl . . . strangled . . . Kettering.' From that I can tell you that you have a picture of the deceased in your wallet . . . you have been carrying it about with you for some time!"

"How the hell do you know that?"

"I am clairvoyant. Take the picture out of your wallet, please, and look at it."

I stood up and began frisking myself for the secretarial wallet that I normally carried in the breast pocket of my suit coat. I had placed a picture of Barbara Butler in it nearly two months before. As far as I could recall I had never used the picture in connection with the murder investigation . . . I had never shown it to anyone except my wife and some personal friends. I couldn't imagine how Dodd knew about the picture.

"You're right about the picture in the wallet," I mumbled into the phone. "But I don't have the wallet with me. . . . I just remembered that I forgot to take it out of another jacket this morning; I can go home and get it if—"

"No matter . . . I can see the picture very clearly. I can tell from the picture that the deceased is white . . . with short dark hair cut close to the head . . . wearing a white sweater . . . not wearing glasses . . . Why, I wonder, did she remove her glasses when the picture was taken?"

"Glasses? Do you mean prescription eyeglasses?"

"Yes!"

"You're wrong about that. The victim didn't wear prescription glasses. But I guess I've got to allow you one error . . . as best as I can recall that picture of the girl, you were right on everything else—except maybe about the sweater . . . I can't remember whether it was a white sweater or a white blouse."

"It is a white sweater," Dodd insisted. (I checked the picture later that evening—Miss Butler was wearing a white sweater in the portrait. The same picture was published several times in the Dayton *Daily News,* so it was possible that Dodd was able to describe it from having seen it in print.) He continued, "And you will find out that I am also correct about the prescription eyeglasses!"

I had never heard anybody—police or acquaintance of the victim—mention anything about Barbara Butler wearing prescription eyeglasses. In fact, I could recall something to the contrary—an apartment-complex employee expressing surprise that a pair of sunglasses had been found on top of the body. The employee had said she had never seen Barbara wearing glasses of any type. But I didn't want to argue the point with Dodd. He had impressed me with his knowledge of the picture and his ability to tell me—over the phone— what a girl looked like in a picture that was inside my wallet in the pocket of a jacket hanging in my bedroom closet at home. I wanted to hear more of what Dodd had to say.

"Glasses are a good subject," I said, trying to find out if Dodd knew anything about the sunglasses. "Do you sense anything about a pair of glasses that are not prescription but might have some connection with the murder?"

After a pause, Dodd responded in a low, deliberate monotone, "I see now a pair of glasses that have dark eyes, but these are not the glasses of which I must speak to you. The other glasses—the pair that are important—have white stems and lenses bordered with rhinestones."

I thought that "glasses with dark eyes" was a peculiar way to describe sunglasses. The other glasses with white stems and rhinestones meant nothing to me. I told Dodd, "If Barbara Butler had a pair of glasses like that, I never heard of them."

"Bar-bar-a!" The sound of the victim's name came softly and slowly into my ear almost as if Dodd had breathed it into the mouthpiece of his phone. I knew that I had told Dodd the victim's name and wondered what use he was going to make of it. I was discouraged when he said, "One of Barbara's eyes did need a prescription—the left eye!"

"Why do you keep talking about prescription eyeglasses?"

"Because you must know of them before I can help you . . . I sense this very deeply."

I wondered if Dodd was trying to tell me something about the case that I didn't know about. But I couldn't imagine what connection a pair of prescription eyeglasses could have with the murder. I decided to wait Dodd out, say nothing, and see how he would react to that.

Dodd broke the long silence by proclaiming in a loud

voice, "Something about when she was deceased . . . I have it now: she was in her cycle of the month!"

"Yes!" I had been hit hard because the fact that Barbara Butler was in her menstrual cycle at death had never been printed or broadcast. A menstrual cycle is—by its very nature—not something that people gossip about; thus I considered it to be an esoteric fact of the murder investigation. Dodd had knowledge of an obscure fact of the case. What else did he know?

"I think we had better continue this conversation on a face-to-face basis," I said. "Where and when can I see you?"

"Actually, I do some of my best work over the phone and on an empty stomach. However, if you insist on seeing me, I will eat supper, wash up, change clothes, and meet you at the *Daily News* office in one hour—at seven o'clock."

"Do you know where the newspaper is? And where to find me here?"

"Mis-ter Clark," I was informed in a tone of voice that exuded both confidence and mockery, "I am clairvoyant! I will find you!"

12

At precisely seven o'clock on the evening of Thursday, August 1, the elevator door opened on the third floor of the *Daily News* building. Out of the elevator stepped a tall, thin young man dressed in a gray suit, white shirt, and conservative tie. He had a pale oval face topped by jet-black hair slicked straight back from a high forehead. His deep-set blue eyes were focused directly on me. He walked, without a moment's hesitation, directly from the elevator door to my desk at the right side of the city room. "Mr. Clark," he said, extending his right hand and flashing me a wide smile, "I am Norman Dodd."

"You're right on time," I said, shaking hands. "Guess you didn't have any trouble finding the place. Ever been here before?"

"No." He looked around the city room before adding,

"And it's too bad about that girl reporter who sits over there someplace—she won't be here much longer."

"What?"

"That dark, Italian-looking girl . . . pretty . . . you do have one that fits that description, don't you?"

"Well, yeah—I guess we do. What about her?"

"Let me see if I can find her desk," he said, turning away from me and walking across the silent city room, his right hand pressed against his forehead in a trancelike gesture. It was long past deadline and I was the only reporter in the large room. I watched, fascinated, as Dodd walked to the desk where a pretty, dark-complexioned single woman in her late twenties sat during working hours. "This is it," he announced, placing the palm of his left hand on the top of the empty desk. "She's pushing thirty," he said, "and a college graduate, too. . . . She should have known better."

"That's the desk," I mumbled, "but what do you mean? What should she have known?"

"Not to get pregnant," Dodd announced. "The man who did it will never marry her and she'll have to quit her job and go away someplace to have the baby."

I did not know what to say or think. Then, from behind me, I heard a roar of laughter. Two nightside photographers had been standing there watching and listening. I gave them a dirty look and motioned for them to get lost. I thought: That girl will scratch my eyes out if those photographers tell her what this guy Dodd has just come out with. (Word of the incident spread about the newspaper, as I feared it would. However, if the young woman in question heard of it, she never mentioned the fact to me. Six weeks later she resigned from the newspaper staff. Her reason for leaving, she said, was to "take a trip around the world.")

I suggested to Dodd that we forget the allegedly pregnant girl and talk, instead, of the murder.

"Ah, yes—the murder. That's what we're here for, isn't it? Pardon me if I get an occasional thought about other matters; it's not intentional, believe me. But when they tell me something, I say it."

"They tell you?"

"Matter of speech. I don't know how or why these things come to me . . . so I just attribute it to 'they.'"

"I see . . . I guess."

"I also pick up vibrations from people who frequent places that I am in. I'm sure that I picked up the pregnant girl's

83

vibrations. That's why I got onto that subject. I hope I don't frighten you if I tell you that I may have to go into a trance in order to rid myself of meaningless vibrations and help you with the murder case. May I sit down?"

"Sure, sure," I replied, showing Dodd to a seat on a couch in the reception area near the elevator. I sat down in a chair opposite him and asked, "If you do go into one of these things—a trance—what do I do? How do I get you back here?"

"Nothing! Do nothing! Just wait! Just relax and I will take care of it myself. I am always able to return from my journeys."

I asked myself: Clark, what have you gotten yourself into?

Dodd pressed the palm of his right hand against his forehead and leaned forward, moaning, "Barbara! Barbara, where are you?"

I thought: Oh, no, this character thinks he can talk to the dead.

A minute passed. Then another. Dodd said nothing although his mouth was open and his eyeballs were revolving about the sockets. I was about to go for help when Dodd shook himself, blinked his eyes, and said:

"No! My trance will not come . . . but I do know that there were two cars involved. . . . The body was found in a small car. . . . There is an older Oldsmobile—or make of car similar to it—also involved."

I picked up a notebook and began writing feverishly—trying to put down on paper every word that came out of Dodd's mouth:

"He's a young man. . . .

"She was a teacher. . . .

"Where she teaches—are there driver-age people at the school?"

I assumed that the first phrase meant the killer, that the second statement was a reference to Barbara Butler, and that the question referred to the junior high school where she taught. I answered his question by saying:

"The teachers at the school could drive, but the pupils would be too young to have had any driver education."

"Check the people driving to that school in an older Oldsmobile . . . I think it's light at the bottom and brown on the top part."

I noted what Dodd said and wondered why he had made a second reference to an older Oldsmobile.

Dodd was quiet a moment, then he took a different tack:

"Three people know of this. Away from the city now—at least one of them is, or was, and came back. Someone went away on a trip recently and came back!"

My mind raced backward to the phone call I had received several days before from my wife's friend Linda Keagan. She had told me about a trip . . . a trip to an out-of-town zoo. She had told me that Kevin Drake, the teacher who had broken up with the victim a week and a half before the murder, had been a chaperon on that trip. I told Dodd, "Someone connected with the Butler case has been on a trip recently. What can you sense about this person?"

Dodd then let loose with a burst of statements, all of them, I thought, applicable to Kevin Drake:

"He has a weakness of the stomach . . . very nervous . . . very tense . . . there are books around him . . . he knows how to use books . . . educated . . . possibly a teacher in his own right . . . this man has an excellent physique—he works out to keep it . . . this man has a beard, or he did have . . . he is very meticulously clean . . . anything filthy or dirty would upset his stomach . . . he was inflamed over a going away . . . a breaking off."

"You've been describing a man I recognize as a onetime suspect in this case," I informed him. "Are you telling me that this person is the killer?"

"I hate to point fingers and say that he did it . . . I may be picking him up because he is grieving . . . but if he did do it . . . kill her . . . if I find this man before you do, I will cause him to turn himself in."

"Wait a minute! Don't try anything like that. Let the police handle that part. The police know who this guy is . . . they've had him in for questioning. I understand he was able to account for his movements on the day of the murder and passed a polygraph examination."

Dodd's eyes flashed. He leaped to his feet, pointed a finger in my face, and said, "Most polygraph questions tend to rely on a yes or no answer. Tell the police to give him another test and ask him this subnormal question: 'Describe a menstrual cycle!' "

"What would that prove?"

"It will trip him up. It will break his train of thought. The person who killed Barbara Butler was able to channel his mind and beat the polygraph. But the menstrual cycle is the key to breaking him. You see, it was the fact that the victim was in her menstrual cycle which prevented the killer from raping her—he wanted to do it, but he couldn't because his stomach became upset at the sight of the blood."

"You may be right," I thought aloud. "Can you tell me this man's name?"

"Names mean nothing to me. . . . Wait! There is a woman! I excluded the woman at first. . . . She is a girl who left . . . a teacher who went away to further her education."

Dodd had switched to the roommate. "Go on," I encouraged him, before asking, "But why do you bring her up now? You just said the killer was a man."

"Don't take me literally on genders . . . I use she and he interchangeably."

Dodd then began to ramble from point to point in a series of disjointed phrases:

"Very short nails . . . a woman's thumb . . . or an unusually shaped man's thumb . . . I see something closely knitted—a sweater, perhaps. . . . Do the police have the victim's mail? I see a love letter type of thing with rough-edge stationery . . . I keep getting this other car—the older Olds . . . I don't know where I get this brown-and-white car from . . . but they changed cars . . . first one, then the other, then back to the first one—The Volkswagen! The body was found in the VW?"

"Yes," I answered. I couldn't recall having mentioned the make of Miss Butler's auto to Dodd. He could have learned this fact, of course, from reading the newspapers, so there was nothing startling about his knowledge of the VW.

"Was the seat in the VW all the way back?"

"I don't know. Why do you want to know?"

"Because I'm trying to find out if she was assaulted in the car or not. The police should have found a fingerprint on the lever that lets the seat back. . . . Did they?"

"I don't believe so."

"Did the police take any brushings from the pedal area?"

"They vacuumed the entire car."

"Was there any evidence of clay in the car?"

"Not that I know of."

"They should have found some from his shoes."

I thought that Dodd was running out of gas. "Are you getting tired?" I asked.

"No."

"Maybe we ought to try again another time."

"*No!* Please be quiet, I may be getting something."

Dodd was silent for several minutes. Then he shouted, "I see something blue!"

I was jolted to attention. Did Dodd know about the small piece of blue terry cloth found in the shopping bag? The police had long wondered if this bit of evidence had any significance. "What about something blue?" I asked.

"It was not logically in the place in which it was found."

"Where was it found?"

"In the car."

"Where in the car?"

Dodd did not reply. There was a look of agony on his face. He seemed to be straining for an answer.

"If you can't sense where, can you sense what? Describe the something blue?"

"A medallion?"

I shook my head negatively, wondering: Is he playing a game with me? Does he know about the piece of blue cloth or doesn't he?

Dodd drifted far off base by asking, "Was she Catholic?"

"No."

"The police went over her car with a fine-tooth comb and found nothing?"

Dodd was talking in questions. Was he pumping me? Was he trying to find out what the police knew and did not know? "Let's say that the police didn't find much in the way of evidence," I answered.

"The bruise marks did not go all the way around the victim's neck!"

"Where were the marks?" I asked.

"Everywhere except . . . except the back of the neck?"

He did not sound sure of himself. Was he probing again? I answered, "You're only part right about the marks."

"No marks on the front of the neck either?"

I nodded.

"A man's thumb! Very short."

I shrugged my shoulders.

"Ask the police if they will accept a pressure point."

"To explain the discontinuous marks?"

"Yes! I see a hand about the throat. The man with this

hand has a very weird and broad knowledge in this particular realm—he knows pressure points, Hindu tactics, karate. The killer used his knowledge of pressure points to find the ones on the front of her neck . . . he applied pressure to one of them and put her unconscious."

"The coroner has ruled that the marks on the sides of the neck were made by some type of thin cord . . . there were no thumb or hand marks."

"They should check the neck again. If they do, they will find that I am right."

"The girl is buried. I doubt that they would exhume her just on the say-so of—"

"A fortuneteller, that's what they will call me. These insults no longer upset me."

"Look, I appreciate your coming down here and talking to me. You've told me some truly remarkable things. Please don't get discouraged. I didn't mean to imply—"

"Mr. Clark, I know what you meant. Do the police have the victim's clothes in polyethylene bags? Don't answer— they do! I see her clothing about her knees when she was found."

"Can you describe the clothing?"

"They were jamaicas as opposed to a dress—something like jamaicas . . . bright, multicolored . . . more colors than one in them."

"God damn, that's good," I encouraged him. "You didn't say culottes or pant-dress—which is the way we described her clothing in print. You said 'something like jamaicas.'"

"I told you on the telephone that I have never read a newspaper account of this case."

"I know what you told me—but that doesn't prove anything. I'm only impressed when you tell me something that I know for certain that you could not have read in a newspaper story or heard on radio or TV. And you just did when you said her culottes were bright and multicolored. Were they ever! Yellow with red, brown, and green floral designs —but nobody ever published a word about the colors of her pant-dress."

"Yes. Now I will tell you something that is very important. When you told me the actual colors of the dress I sensed these numbers: five, four, three."

"What about them?"

"The time five-forty-three is very important to this case."

88

"The body was found about a half hour before that time. Do you think she was killed at five-forty-three?"

"Perhaps."

"The coroner says she couldn't have died before eight o'clock—but your time fits in a lot better with a theory the police have that the victim was abducted from the parking lot and murdered several hours before eight o'clock on Wednesday, June 12."

"I see," Dodd said and began pacing about the room. "Were her hands bound behind her back?"

Again I wasn't sure if Dodd was asking a question or stating a fact. I answered him by saying, "Her arms were bound, but the police don't know whether they were taped together up against her chest or behind her back."

"Were her hands free when they found her?"

"Yes."

"Were there marks on her wrists?"

"On one wrist, yes. Marks from where the tape had been. The tape was still on her left wrist but the loop that had been on the right wrist had been pulled free—either by the girl in her death agony or by the killer."

"I should like to feel the tape. But I can tell you now that her hands were bound behind her back. The dress was on her at death. The hands then had to be pulled free of the tape in order to undress her. They started to pull the dress off, but couldn't with the arms tied behind the back, so they pulled an arm free of the tape."

"You said 'they'?"

"Matter of speech again. Now I will show you what happened." Dodd stretched out on the couch and placed his arms behind his back as if they were bound.

"I see the arms falling free like this!" he shouted, as his arms flopped into a position in front of his chest. He clenched his fists. His head came down until his jaw rested against his throat. He spread his legs at a 45-degree angle to one another and then bent them back at the knees until his feet touched his buttocks.

I could hardly believe my eyes: Dodd had forced his body into the same position that I had seen Barbara Butler's body in on color slides of the death scene shown me by the coroner.

"I am on the floor of the Volkswagen," Dodd announced. "I must go back further . . . back to the store. I see her walking in the store," he said, jumping up. He walked off

89

down an aisle between newsroom desks. "She gets this . . . she gets this," he said, plucking imaginary items from imaginary shelves as he went. Then he stopped, turned around, walked back to me, and said, "Her pocketbook—I see it. Was it a brown-colored wicker-type purse with a stable handle and hinges that allow the purse to swing?"

"That's just the way I would describe Barbara Butler's purse. Are you able to read my mind or something?"

"I sense things—I don't read minds. There was something frilly on the pocketbook."

"I don't think so."

"Forget it. She had been wandering about the store killing time. She bought something in a can with an unpleasant odor to it—a drain remover or unclogger or something like that?"

"Well," I allowed, "she bought something along that line."

"A liquid soap in a plastic container?"

"She bought cleaning supplies in order to strip-wax the floors in her apartment."

"Yes," Dodd agreed in a voice that implied that I had taken the words out of his mouth. "But when she went through the checkout line, she still didn't see the other party. She met the individual outside the store."

"When you say 'individual' and 'other party'—you mean the killer!"

"Yes! But before that—at the checkout counter—she had an expression on her face that you or I wouldn't normally have at a store . . . she had an expression of being very concerned about something."

"Do you know why Barbara Butler was upset at the checkout counter?"

"I see her taking a wallet out of her purse. . . . She fumbled for change and came up with the right amount."

I stared at Dodd in my best poker face. I didn't know what to make of what he had just told me. He had been so right on so many things and now he had just told me that the victim had paid for her purchases in cash when, in fact, the reason for her being upset was that she had a problem getting the store to accept her check.

"Would a dollar and some change cover it?" Dodd asked.

I shook my head slowly from side to side.

"Would two one-dollar bills do it, then? It couldn't be over three dollars, because I don't see her having a large amount of things in front of her."

"She didn't have many items, but their cost was quite a bit more than three dollars."

"Was there a box?" Dodd asked.

"You tell me," I answered, knowing that it was common knowledge in the Dayton area that there was a box and that the box contained an outdoor charcoal grill.

"I see a bottle, a can, and a box," Dodd said with some conviction in his voice. "I see a look of preoccupation about her. I see concern—she is more concerned with future dealings than those of the moment."

There was a pause.

Dodd resumed by saying, "I don't see her with a smile on her face when she went through that line. She's very preoccupied . . . very concerned . . . but I can't put my finger on the concern."

"You said a few minutes ago that Barbara met her killer outside the store. Who did she meet? Can you sense anything at all about this person?"

"I did, but I don't now . . . I can no longer see this party. I can only tell you that the body of the girl was not abused at the store. It was done somewhere else and her body brought back to the store."

"Where was she killed? This is very important."

Dodd stared off into space for several minutes without saying a word or moving a muscle. Then he slowly began to shake his head. "I'm afraid I'm losing it," he mumbled. "My powers are weakening."

"Let's try something else. Do you sense anything at all about a woman who may know something about this case?"

"A woman . . . no!"

"This woman's conscience may be bothering her. . . . She made a mysterious phone call to one of our reporters the other day saying she wanted to talk about the murder. . . . She broke off the conversation without revealing her name. . . . Her last words were, 'Someone is coming into the office, I've got to hang up.' "

Dodd looked stunned. "Office! Yes! Real estate office."

"You sense that the woman works in a real estate office?"

"Yes! A woman called one of your police reporters earlier this week. I don't think she knows anything. Just wanted to talk to someone. She works in a real estate office located near the Ontario Store lot—on the north side of the parking lot."

"Wait a minute," I said. "That can't be right. There's

nothing on the north side of that parking lot except a cement wall. I've been there enough times to know that."

For perhaps five minutes Dodd sat slumped down on the couch with a look of pathetic helplessness on his face.

"Maybe I've pushed you too hard," I said. "Let's get together again some other time. How about Saturday morning?"

"Yes, Saturday morning—when I'm not so drained from working all day. Come to my home when you are ready."

Without another word Dodd stood up, strode across the city room to the elevator, and disappeared.

I went home that night in a mood that I can only describe in retrospect as being one of interested confusion. I was most certainly impressed by the many things Dodd had told me that I knew to be correct. He had said nothing to indicate to me that he was a phony of Mrs. Beatrice Cook's ilk. He had made only one bad mistake—the bit about the eyeglasses. In general, though, if he hadn't "sensed" anything about a particular subject, he had admitted as much without resorting to obvious bluffs. However, my feeling of wonder about the range of Dodd's knowledge (and the ways he expressed it) was conditioned by an inability to believe that any human being can obtain information "out of the ether!" I thought of Dodd as I had often thought of the murder. he was a mystery for which there was a reasonable answer somewhere. I expected to find at least a hint of the rational explanation as to the source of Dodd's knowledge from Lieutenant Horn at the Kettering police station the following day.

13

We were about ten minutes into the briefing when Detective Lieutenant Al Horn interrupted me by asking, "What was that you just said about eyeglasses?"

"I said this guy Dodd gets way off base sometimes—like, he tried to tell me that Barbara Butler wore prescription eyeglasses."

The detective and I were seated across from each other

on swivel chairs in the inner office of the Kettering detective section. Horn had a legal-size notebook cradled in his lap. He tapped a pencil against the binding of the pad several times. Then he said, "I think we better get a few things straight before you read me back any more notes of your meeting last night with Mr. Dodd. You know what the death scene looked like and what evidence we found inside the Volkswagen, don't you?"

"Yes. I saw the color slides taken at the scene by the coroner's man. You people here in Kettering told me the rest of what I know."

"Okay. Now I must ask you to tell me exactly what items, to your knowledge, were found in the victim's purse?"

I thought a moment before answering. "A key chain . . . a wallet containing a small amount of change and her personal papers . . . some sales receipts . . . and the glass case for her sunglasses."

Horn gave me a long suspicious stare before saying, "All right, now tell me what Dodd told you about prescription glasses."

"He claimed she wore a pair of white-stemmed glasses with rhinestone decorations on them. I guess he meant by that that rhinestones are where the temples and frames join. I know he said that she only needed a prescription for her left eye."

For perhaps thirty seconds the lieutenant glared at me without a sign of emotion on his rugged features. I wasn't stupid; I had started to guess something of what was coming and a shiver of anticipation ran down my spine. I returned Horn's stare; the next move was up to him. The silence in the room was broken by a squeaking sound as Horn began to rock his body slowly back and forth in his chair. Then he grunted, spun about in the chair, stood up, and walked over to a file cabinet. He stuck his hand in his right pants pocket, pulled out a key chain, and fumbled over it for a key to the file cabinet. He unlocked the cabinet, pulled open the bottom drawer, reached a hand into a brown envelope, and pulled out a pair of feminine eyeglasses with opaque temples and frames and rhinestone decorations. He showed me the glasses and asked, "Who do you suppose these belonged to?"

"Barbara Butler?"

"Who else? I'm almost afraid to look," he added, holding the glasses up to an overhead light and peering through first the left lens and then the right. He sighed and handed the glasses to me, saying, "Look for yourself."

I looked through the left lens and my vision was blurred.

I looked through the right lens and my vision was perfect.

The prescription in Barbara Butler's eyeglasses was for the left eye only!

14

The eyeglasses had been found by the police inside the victim's handbag on the floor of the death car.

An officer had looked through the lenses and noted that the prescription in them was comparatively weak and for the left eye only. Acting on a hunch (later verified by the victim's friends) that Barbara Butler would seldom have needed to wear such a pair of glasses, police took the glasses from the scene to their Kettering headquarters and locked them up in a file cabinet. Police then assumed that knowledge of the fact that the victim owned such a pair of glasses was restricted to officers in their department, the family, and close friends of the victim and possibly—if he had gone through the victim's handbag—the killer.

Norman Dodd not only knew of the glasses' existence—he knew that there was a prescription in the left lens and no prescription in the right lens.

My initial reaction was that Dodd had proved himself to be clairvoyant. "He's got to be!" I exclaimed. "How else could he have known that the prescription is in the left lens only?" I shuddered when it dawned on me that Dodd could have learned about the prescription the same way that the detective and I had: by looking through the lenses! Or he could have been told about the prescription by someone else who had had an opportunity to look through those lenses. The more I thought about it the more I came to realize that Dodd could be many things. Among them:

(1) A clairvoyant as he claimed to be.

(2) A person previously acquainted with Barbara Butler.

(3) A person acquainted with Kevin Drake—with a probable ax to grind against Drake.

94

(4) A person with a close contact in the Kettering Police Department who was feeding him information. (I also realized that the Kettering police could suspect me of being in collusion with Dodd to deceive them. I stated this point in a memo to Kettering police summarizing my opinions of Dodd following my first contact with him.)

(5) Not a true clairvoyant, but a very perceptive person able to study the photograph of another and discern from some key (how the eye is focused or shaped) that the person whose portrait he's looking at requires an eyeglass prescription.

(6) An exceptional crank who had made a study of the victim, the case, and—at least to the point of knowing I carried a picture of the victim in my wallet—myself.

Now, if Dodd was only number one—a clairvoyant—then I had to look at him as being a rare and exceptional human being possessed with incredible mental powers that very well might enable him to solve the murder mystery.

If he was any one (or any combination) of the other possibilities, then he was playing some kind of dangerous game for which neither Lieutenant Horn nor I knew the rules.

From a personal standpoint, things became even more confusing when I finished reading back all of my notes on the first session with Dodd and learned from Horn that: "Dodd hit on something else besides the eyeglasses that you don't know about."

When I asked what the other "hit" was, the detective conditioned his previous remark by saying, "Dodd wasn't exactly on the mark, but he came close to telling you something about a person we have had doubts about as far as his being one of our honest citizens." Horn refused to explain himself further on the grounds that "If we accept the idea that Dodd has extrasensory perception, we also have to accept the idea that he can read your mind. I don't want you to lead Dodd. . . . I want to see if he will come back to this person on his own."

The possibility that Dodd could read my mind was anything but a comforting thought. (Could this man sense my innermost thoughts? Even any suspicions I might have about him?) However, I decided to go ahead. I was convinced, now, that Dodd was an unusual individual deserving of my undivided attention. (Mrs. Hester Jones Grant—the other name given me by Mrs. Seckinger—was set aside for possible future reference only.)

I thought I should attempt to learn as much as possible about Dodd—a man I now hoped was going to help solve the mystery. However, a check into his background produced little information. His parents were among the small army of Southern mountain people who had drifted north for employment purposes during World War II and settled in the Dayton area. Dodd's grades in elementary and high school were, at best, low-average—and he had managed to score only 85 on an IQ test. He was married and his children were two girls and one boy. He had no military-service record. He did, however, have a satisfactory work record on an assembly line in one of Dayton's largest factories, where he worked an early-morning to early-afternoon shift alongside thousands of other wage earners. He resided in a Dayton suburb not far from his place of employment and his work hours would have permitted him to return home from work at least an hour before 5 P.M. (Mrs. Seckinger had insisted that Dodd "never gets home until after five.") He had no criminal record.

I thought I had no other choice than to take Dodd at face value—a person who was trying to help solve the case. After all, Dodd had only done what he had been asked to do: perceive obscure facts of the case in order to indicate clairvoyant ability. But had he done this too well? Too fast? Too easily? I could not answer these questions because I did not know how genuine clairvoyants (if there were such people) functioned . . . what type of information they were likely to get . . . how they conveyed their information . . . and in what volume. Lieutenant Horn knew no more about these matters than I did. I told Horn that I thought we needed expert help and advice and that the only source of such advice would be a parapsychologist.

A parapsychologist is defined as a specialist in the branch of science concerned with the investigation by experimental means of a person's contact with his environment without the use of his senses and muscles. This exchange may be extrasensory perception (telepathy, clairvoyance or precognition). Or it may be psychokinesis, the action of "mind over matter."

Dr. J. B. Rhine, director of the Foundation for Research on the Nature of Man (FRNM) at Durham, North Carolina, is perhaps the world's foremost parapsychologist. His experiments at Duke University (which began in 1928) attracted worldwide attention and gained parapsychology at least a measure of acceptance as a genuine science. Dr. Rhine (Ph.D., Chicago, 1925) did, in fact, introduce the term "extrasensory perception" in one of his numerous books dealing with the results of his research into previously unexplored areas of the mind.

I decided that if anyone could analyze Norman Dodd's clairvoyant abilities and tell me how to proceed with him, that man would be Dr. Rhine.

I telephoned Dr. Rhine and told him the story of my involvement with the alleged clairvoyant. I said that, although I was amazed by the things that Dodd could tell me, I was still not convinced that there could be such a thing as extrasensory perception. I did not expect that this remark would earn me any points with Dr. Rhine, who was then approaching his seventy-third birthday and had devoted the majority of his life to a study of extrasensory perception. Dr. Rhine's response surprised me. I learned that his approach to ESP was still entirely scientific when he said, "I can't make up my own mind as well as I would like about what it is and I have spent over forty years seeking an answer."

Rhine said that he believed that there were "many people in the world with the ability to perceive matters beyond the range of ordinary perception." However, he added that "it has become increasingly difficult in recent years for the layman to know what to accept because of the publication of so many unreliable books and articles on the subject. Also there are still plenty of charlatans taking advantage of credulous peolpe."

Dr. Rhine wanted to know if I had been able to verify that Dodd was gainfully employed. I replied that this had been done and that "as far as I know, he isn't using these alleged psychic powers of his for profit." Rhine said that this was a "good sign if it is true." He then said that Dodd's knowledge of the victim's eyeglass prescription and the fact that she was in her menstrual cycle looked good at face value. No evidence could be conclusive in such a case but this type is the more impressive—encouraging further investigation.

I told Rhine that Dodd had stated both of those facts over the telephone. Rhine said, "It is not likely that a

97

genuine clairvoyant could work over the phone. Although the bit about the eye and the menstrual cycle is impressive, your man could have loaded up on this information if he is clever and experienced at making himself appear to be clairvoyant. You must be very guarded about this man. The modesty—the insistence that his efforts not be publicized—is a sign of a good clairvoyant. . . . It is also good cover for a fake.

"Clairvoyants will often act very cryptic," Rhine explained. "Much of their best information will be provided in statements phrased in the form of a question. The questions indicate the vague way in which the information comes to them. They will appear half unconscious at times and do strange-appearing things. . . . They will mix up both the truth and the facts because they can't tell themselves what they are doing or what they are getting."

I told Dr. Rhine that Dodd had acted this way and had been wrong on some things—that he had known that the victim had a problem at the checkout counter but did not know that it was over a check, and that Dodd had not known that the box contained a barbecue even though this fact had been widely publicized. Rhine said, "I would be more inclined to be certain he was a fake if he only told you correct information."

I then presented this problem: "Dr. Rhine, so far Dodd has pretty much limited himself to telling things about the case that we can check on to see if he is right or wrong. . . . Is there any way that we can evaluate information that he may provide about areas of the case that are a mystery to everyone—such as where the victim went after she left the store?"

Rhine answered that Dodd was "not yet ready for testing. I have a test that you and the police can give him when the proper time comes. If that is successful, we will bring him to Durham for closer study. In the meantime I would say you should continue to work with him. You will never find out what he is if you don't. . . . There may be more to this than just solving a murder mystery. This person could be very important to all of us in the future if he is a genuine clairvoyant. So unless you have overwhelming doubts about him and his information, try to accept him for what he may be—a genuine clairvoyant. If he is genuine, he will continue to provide information; if he is a loaded-up fake, he won't be able to continue to keep giving you information. Now, genuine clairvoyants get discouraged very easily—you and the police have got to encourage this man if you ever hope that he will be able to help you. Try to help him. Work with him with a positive approach . . . don't attempt to make judgments or publicize his efforts until you know much more about him and what he can do. Although I remind you again of your need for caution, I am more impressed by the little you have told me about this man than I usually am by these stories. We will open a file on this man and this case here at the laboratory. I have the feeling that you people might find you have a tremendous story here."

Genuine clairvoyant or loaded-up fake? If the subject matter upon which the answer to this question was going to be based had been either a search for a missing child or some lost valuable object, I would have continued to work with Dodd without a great deal of concern over the consequences as to the truth of the matter. In a murder case, however, the alternatives were terrible to think about: Dodd might be either a saint or a satan. If he was clairvoyant, he might solve the murder mystery . . . if he was a fake, he might have been involved in the creation of the mystery. I had to find out which. Although the very idea of clairvoyancy was still illogical to me, I believed that it was even more illogical to think that Dodd, with an IQ of only 85, had had something to do with Barbara Butler's murder . . . had influenced Mrs. Seckinger to write a letter suggesting the use of clairvoyancy . . . and then had waited six weeks for me—and only me—to fall into some kind of trap, for which I could not see the trip, in order to pose as a clairvoyant.

I went forward into the unknown with only one guide: Dodd *had* to continue to provide information! His failure to do so would be my only warning signal.

15

The second contact, on Saturday, August 3, was a wild affair in which Dodd "sensed things" on a wide variety of subjects ranging from my own suspicions of him to the murder victim's abduction from the Ontario Store parking lot.

I went to Dodd's home, a small suburban ranch, and told him that the police were "quite impressed" with his clairvoyant abilities. I admitted that I had been "stunned when I found out you were right about the victim's eyeglass prescription."

"I hope I wasn't too good in getting that," Dodd reacted. "I mean, I hope you don't think that I'm the killer. You have been wondering about that possibility, haven't you? Don't lie when you answer because I can tell whenever someone lies to me."

"What can I say?" I mumbled, feeling quite embarrassed.

Dodd introduced me to his family. His wife appeared to be a pleasant, attractive young woman, in her midtwenties. His three children were polite and well-groomed. Then Dodd astounded me by telling me some things about my family. I wore a wedding band so he could have known from observation that I was married. But I had no idea how he knew what he did about my six-months-pregnant wife, Charlotte. "Your wife has been talking to someone about the new baby," Dodd said. "She has worries about it. . . . Tell her not to worry . . . everything will be all right and it will be a girl just like your first child." (Our second daughter was born by natural childbirth, without problems, on November 26, 1968.)

My wife, a twin herself, had been concerned about the possibility of having twins on her second pregnancy in two years. She had mentioned this to me and others, including our family doctor, in recent weeks. I was still wondering how Dodd knew this when he asked and answered this question: "Has your wife bought those shoes yet? I don't think so."

I told Dodd that I didn't know what he was talking about. Dodd insisted that "she tried on a pair of reddish-colored shoes in a store yesterday . . . but didn't buy them."

Dayton *Daily News* Managing Editor Greg Favre had been told about Dodd and wanted to meet him. I suggested to Dodd that we go to the newspaper in my car, pick Favre up there, and then attempt to reconstruct Barbara Butler's fatal June 12 trip from her apartment to the Ontario Discount Store. "Just let me wash up a bit, put on a tie and suit coat," Dodd insisted, "and I'll be ready to go." Dodd had said something similar to me over the phone when he agreed to the first meeting at the newspaper. The young factory worker's insistence upon being well-scrubbed and well-dressed before attempting to work on the murder case was interesting; his attitude was almost that of a surgeon preparing for an operation.

We drove to downtown Dayton. I parked my car in a no-parking zone in front of the newspaper building. We went inside the building. The managing editor was busy with a problem concerning the first edition. Dodd and I exchanged some small talk while we waited. From out of the blue Dodd advised me, "You better go move your car because there's a cop coming down the street." When he issued his warning, Dodd was standing in a corner of the newsroom where he had no view of the street three floors below. I went outside, looked up the street, and saw a policeman ticketing another car. I moved my car.

I went back to Dodd and asked him if he would "like to go to the race track someday? I'd like to play a few of your hunches!"

"I don't use my powers for profit," Dodd replied, "except in the export business."

I asked him to explain what he meant by that.

"I went into a trance one day last spring and got the feeling that some parties in Europe needed items that I could supply them with. I wrote these people and we have since entered into a business arrangement. I will tell you more about it if it works out. In fact, you may even find that you will want to write a book about me and my accomplishments someday."

This bothered me. Dodd was not as opposed to publicity and profit as he had indicated earlier.

Favre joined us. I introduced Dodd to my boss and we prepared to leave the building.

Dodd, Favre, and I stepped into the elevator. Favre was about to push a button which would close the elevator doors and cause the car to descend to street level when Dodd shouted, "Don't do it! You can't leave! Something's going to happen!"

Favre and I stared at each other. I don't know what the managing editor thought, but I wondered if the car was going to crash into the basement. It was not a humorous thought.

101

A second or two later, a copyboy shouted at us from across the city room, "Mr. Favre! Wait! Don't go—there's a phone call for you."

"Take a message," Favre replied. "I'll call whoever it is back later." He pushed the door-close button.

Dodd reached over and pushed the door-open button, causing the half-closed elevator doors to snap open.

"What did you do that for?" Favre asked.

"Because the phone call is important—you've got to answer it!"

"I get a lot of phone calls," Favre said. "What's so important about this one?"

Dodd didn't have to answer the question; the copyboy did it for him by yelling, "Mr. Favre, Mr. Fain calling from Florida—he's got to talk to you!"

Favre returned to his office to take the phone call from his superior—*Daily News* editor Jim Fain, who was in Miami at the time covering the 1968 Republican National Convention.

We drove to the Woodman Park Drive Apartments and parked in the now-paved parking lot in front of the former Butler-Gray apartment. We were in luck—a man was in the process of moving into the apartment, which had been vacant since the murder. I identified myself to the man and asked if Dodd, whom I described as being a clairvoyant, might "look around inside." The man, who knew of the former tenant's fate, not only agreed to this, he asked to be permitted to follow us around the apartment in order to "hear what the clairvoyant says. I just finished reading a book about clairvoyancy," he added. "That stuff fascinates me."

We went into the apartment and then upstairs. Dodd correctly sensed that the two roommates had used only one of the two upstairs bedrooms as a sleeping room and that the other bedroom had been used for storage. However, he named the storage room as the sleeping room and the sleeping room as a storage room. The apartment was cluttered with boxes containing the possessions of the man who was moving in. Dodd said that "there was a lot of stuff in boxes around this apartment the day that the victim was last here." I assumed that he had correctly sensed that Miss Butler's roommate had her possessions packed and ready to move out on the day of the murder.

Dodd spent a considerable amount of time wandering from room to room and peeking in empty closets. He ran the palms of his hands over the apartment walls and eventually concluded, "It didn't happen here . . . this is not the place. . . . She went from here to the store but never returned."

We were standing at the top of the staircase when Dodd smiled and exclaimed, "I have her now! Follow me and note what I do. I couldn't pick her up before because I thought she was in a serious mood . . . she wasn't . . . she was happy . . . very girlish."

Dodd then faced the wall of the stairwell and skipped down the stairs, shouting, "This is the way she came down these stairs the day she died! She hopped downstairs sideways whenever she was happy!"

My last recollection of the new occupant of apartment 9 was of a very confused man standing at the top of the stairs and scratching his head.

I scampered down the stairs after Dodd and followed him across the living room to the door leading outside. This was a crucial point: would he know that the victim's car was *not* parked in the lot in front of that door on the day of the murder or wouldn't he?

Dodd knew! He went out the door, turned to his right, and walked about a hundred yards to the east and down a grassy slope to the area where Miss Butler's neighbors said that her car was parked before she went to the store.

"Why am I drawn to this place?" Dodd asked. "Logically she would have parked up there by her apartment. Why was her car down here?"

I told Dodd that the parking lot adjoining the apartment was not in use on the day of the murder because the driveway into it was being paved. "I'm very impressed," I added, "by the way you seem to be able to get the sense of things that happened without knowing exactly why they happened. I only hope you can do as well over in the Ontario Store parking lot. You wait here and I'll go back up and get my car. Then we'll see if you can follow the victim from here to the place in the lot where the car and body were discovered."

Now, this would not be a very difficult assignment for a loaded-fake. From reading the newspapers a fake would know that the victim stopped at the rental office on her way out of the apartment complex to apply for a pool pass. If a fake had familiarized himself with the route between the apartment complex and the store, he would know that the victim would have had to use Woodman Drive for half of her journey to the store and then make a decision at the intersection of Woodman and Patterson Road as to which of two possible routes to take from that point to the store. And if a fake had spent any amount of time in the store parking lot he would know that the only parking space in the lot with a huge glob of dried white paint in the middle of it was the place where the car and body were discovered.

As I began the five-mile drive from the victim's apartment to the store—with Dodd in the front seat beside me and Favre observing from the back seat—I had no idea what the clairvoyant would do with this situation. I thought that I could no longer be surprised by anything that he might do—but I was! He did not sense that the victim stopped at the rental office . . . he did sense the need for the victim to make a route decision at the Woodman-Patterson intersection, but he did not know which choice she made. . . . He announced along the way that I should stop if we came upon a dry-cleaning plant "because I feel that the victim went into a dry-cleaning store to pick up some clothing shortly before she died." (This was true—but it happened not in the Dayton area on the day of the murder but in Columbus at her father's dry-cleaning plant on the day before.) Then, at the Ontario Store, the following occurred:

I drove slowly onto the huge, four-acre parking lot. I looked at Dodd and asked, "Which way do you want me to go—left, right, straight ahead, or what?"

"Keep to the right and go up near the store."

He had directed me toward the area of the lot where the victim's car and body were discovered.

"Straight now, this is the correct row."

"This is the row of parking spaces in which the VW was found," I agreed. "What are you going to do—direct me to the exact spot?"

"I shall try. . . . Would you be impressed if I came close?"

"Well, there are about two thousand parking spaces in this lot—I guess I would have to be impressed if you came close to picking one spot out of two thousand without any prior knowledge of the correct location."

"Do you know the exact spot?" Dodd asked.

"Yes . . . and so do a lot of people who shop here."

Dodd frowned.

"Slow down," he said as we approached the correct spot. "It's right around here somewhere."

I nodded. The correct space was vacant and clearly marked by the paint spot. I pulled into it, turned off the car engine, and looked at Dodd. He gave me a quizzical stare in return, but said nothing. The he got out of the car, walked four parking spaces away from the correct one, and announced, "I'll say this is it."

"What about the space where I parked?"

"I should have known," Dodd mumbled. "It was the only vacant parking place around here. . . . People avoid parking there 'cause they know it's where the body was found."

"Do you think the victim parked in that space when she came to the store on the afternoon of June 12?"

"No . . . the killer left the car over here. . . . The victim parked in another place that afternoon."

"What other place?"

"Where is the playground?"

"The playground? There's no playground around here. Why did you ask that question?"

"Because I hear this zzzzzzzzzing sound."

"I don't hear anything."

"No! Of course you don't. But I hear it. I hear what Barbara heard. It sounds like a . . . like a model airplane. That's it! Where is the flat open space around here . . . a playground or something . . . where a boy could fly a model airplane?"

"Well, this parking lot is big enough to fly a model airplane around in. . . ."

"No! I don't mean the parking lot. . . . I need to find a flat open space near this lot."

"There are some fields out in back of the store . . . is that what you're talking about?"

"No! There's a playground nearby. I must find it!"

I looked around the lot: to the west I saw Wilmington Pike—a street filled with traffic and bordered by business establishments; to the south I saw a grassy incline topped by a wholesale beer outlet and the backsides of other buildings which fronted on another street farther to the south; to the east I saw the store itself; to the north I saw a high cement wall, indicating to me that there was little chance of a playground in that direction.

"No playground around here," I said. "If there is . . . I don't know where it would be."

"I will find it," Dodd insisted. "First, we'll go into the store. . . . I'll pick up Barbara's trail there and let her lead me back out to the place where her car was parked in the lot."

Dodd spent the best part of an hour strolling about the interior of the Ontario Store; his powers of perception were the same on the actual scene as they had been two nights before in the *Daily News* city room: he sensed that the victim purchased cleaning supplies but could not sense that she purchased a barbecue and that her problem at the checkout counter was over a check. I decided that these facts were unimportant compared to what Dodd might be able to sense outside the store. I told him about the barbecue and the check to eliminate any possibility that he might be thrown off by his lack of knowledge in these areas. Dodd's reaction was mixed: he was pleased that he had "come pretty close on the check. I knew she had a problem at the checkout counter—I just couldn't put my finger on what it was about"; he was depressed that he had "missed the barbecue—I can't understand how that could have happened," he moaned. "We walked right through the barbecue department and I didn't sense a thing there." Dodd asked, "Are you positive that she bought a barbecue?" I told him that the victim bought a small hibachi barbecue and that it was found on the back seat of her car inside its box. With that, Dodd turned on his heels and walked back to the barbecue department. He returned a few minutes later with a look of satisfaction on his face. "I know why I didn't get it before," he announced. "They don't have any hibachi barbecues left in stock—if there had been one here I would have sensed that the victim bought one."

We went back outside. Dodd began acting extremely agitated the second that he was in the parking lot. He turned to his right and began to walk in a northerly direction, or toward the side of the parking lot opposite from where the car and body had been discovered. "I am drawn this way," he mumbled; "the victim came this way."

He continued on until he came to the wall bounding the north side of the parking lot. He repeated his earlier contention that he was "looking for a flat open space to fly a model airplane."

I leaned against the wall and watched Dodd wander aimlessly up and down rows of parking spaces. After several minutes of this I got restless and grasped the top of the wall with my hands and pulled myself up so that I could peer over it. I was so startled by what I saw on the other side of that wall that I lost my grip and dropped back down onto the parking lot pavement. "There's your God-damned playground," I shouted. "It's right there on the other side of this wall!"

"I knew it!" Dodd exclaimed. "She was parked right around here someplace, then . . . I hear this zzzzzzzzing sound . . . the same sound she heard when she returned to her car from the store . . . a young boy was on the other side of that wall flying a model plane at the time."

"You feel that the victim was attacked right here?" I asked.

"She met someone here . . . the brown or tannish Olds-mobile was parked nearby. . . ."

I assumed that Dodd had "come back" to the other "hit" that Lieutenant Horn had mentioned the day before.

Dodd took a few steps back toward the store and then stopped. He reeled backward, grabbed the right side of his face, and shrieked as if he were in agony.

"What the hell! What's the matter?" I yelled.

"Any bruises on her face? The victim . . . was she hit on the right side of her face?"

"She had a black eye," I told him, trying to remember whether it was the left eye or the right eye.

"Which eye? I felt a stunning blow—my teeth hurt—when I walked into that parking space right there." Dodd pointed to the fourth stall in the third row of parking spaces in from the north side of the lot.

"It was the right eye that was black," I said, "I'm sure about it now. Who hit her? What happened next?"

"Someone hit her right here . . . I don't know who . . . but she left the lot with him in her car and then . . ."

He was silent for several seconds. "What then?" I asked, full of impatience. "Don't lose it now . . . what happened next?"

A puzzled expression came over Dodd's face. He sighed and then asked, "When do they sweep the lot?"

"What?" I yelled. "Why do you ask a stupid question like that at a time like this?"

"Because if they swept the lot on the night of the murder, the man who does the work may have seen something important—he may have seen the killer bring the car and body back to the lot."

Dodd insisted that we had to find out about this possibility immediately.

We went inside the store and talked to the manager. Dodd seemed quite relieved when the manager informed us that the lot was swept only on Tuesday and Thursday evenings. The murder occurred on a Wednesday, so there was no chance that a sweeping-equipment operator could have seen "something important," as Dodd had put it. I wondered a good deal about this because there was no reason for a genuine clairvoyant to be as concerned about this point as Dodd had appeared to me to be.

I tried to get Dodd back on the crucial issue of what had happened to Barbara Butler after she left the lot with the person who had hit her in the right eye. He balked at doing this, saying that he could "go no further with that at this time. Let me rest a few days and then I will tell you if I can. I can only tell you now that when the killer is brought in you will find out that he frequents a health spa somewhere in this vicinity in order to practice his body-building exercises."

Greg Favre returned to the newspaper building. I took Dodd to the Kettering police station and introduced him to Lieutenant Horn. Dodd was permitted to touch the pant-dress worn by the victim on the day of the murder, but sensed nothing from this other than his previously expressed opinion that the pant-dress was ripped off the victim after death.

Outside the police station I told Dodd that I was certain that the police attached considerable significance to his repeated references to a "brown Oldsmobile." Dodd said, "Oh?" I asked him to concentrate on the car. I was seeking enough information about the car to permit me to check the ownership with the motor vehicle bureau. Dodd dashed any hopes I had along these lines by saying, "I'm not sure that it's an Olds. It's a brown or tan car that may look like an Olds—a similar GM make, perhaps."

I drove Dodd home and then went to my own apartment. I mixed myself a drink and tried to forget my day with Dodd. But I couldn't. Dodd had continued to provide information, yet he really had gone no further toward a solution of the murder on the second contact that he had on the first. His stopping point both times was the abduction of Miss Butler from the parking lot. There was a barrier of some sort at that point and I was not at all certain that it was due to mental exhaustion, as Dodd had implied.

I was sitting in the living room of our apartment and about halfway into a second martini when I turned to my wife and asked, "Honey, you haven't been trying on any red shoes lately, have you?"

"Red shoes! I tried on a pair yesterday. They were red- dish-orange, actually. But I didn't buy them. Who told you? How did you know?"

I sighed before answering, "Because I've been with a clairvoyant all day. . . . I've got to stop doubting that Dodd. . . . He must have ESP!"

16

On Thursday, August 8, I phoned Dr. J. B. Rhine in Durham and had a long conversation with him about Norman Dodd. That evening I tried, without suc- cess, to reach Dodd by phone to arrange a third meeting. Dodd's phone rang busy over a four-hour period. I checked with the phone company and was told that Dodd's phone was apparently out of order due to cable trouble caused by a storm.

On Friday, August 9, Dodd's phone continued to ring busy throughout the day. About 5:00 P.M. I asked the telephone company repair service to confirm that the prob- lem with Dodd's phone was cable trouble. I was told that Dodd's phone was "apparently off the hook." I became quite concerned for Dodd's welfare. Surely, I thought, a clairvoyant's phone couldn't be off the hook for nearly twenty-four hours without his knowing about it. Had some- one found out that Dodd was providing information about the murder and done something to prevent further dis- closures?

I went to Dodd's home and found him and his family well. Dodd was unaware that his phone was out of order, but he did know that I had been "doing a lot of talking" about him "with another party" the day before. I told Dodd that I had been discussing his clairvoyant abilities with Dr. Rhine. At first Dodd claimed that he had never heard of Rhine. But a minute later Dodd asked, "This guy from Duke, ever seen him?" I said that I had seen and heard Dr. Rhine lecture in Syracuse, New York, several years before. Dodd then described Rhine to me in about the same terms as I recalled him. Dodd appeared very pleased with himself and "took off" on several matters relating to Dr. Rhine that only the ESP expert himself could be the judge of:

"Dr. Rhine . . . he's very conscious of his feet. They are either bothering him or . . . [Dodd did not complete the phrase] Does he have any trouble with his left ear? He may have a tendency to pull at it when he talks. He strokes his face."

I told Dodd that I would write Dr. Rhine and "ask him about these things." Dodd seemed gratified. Then he said that he had "received a sign" that told him his powers were at a peak. "My wife and I have been awakened in the middle of the night several times recently by a red light shining in our bedroom. Last night they told me a word to say to make the light go away. I said this word and the light disappeared."

This was utter nonsense to me. I glanced at Dodd's wife to note her reaction. She smiled and nodded her approval to what her husband had just said.

Dodd announced that he would "answer some questions about the murder case that you [meaning me] have long wondered about." He then provided what I considered to be plausible explanations as to why Barbara Butler's killer took the keys to her car off the key chain and as to how her car and body were returned to the Ontario Store parking lot:

"The car keys were on a dangly thing. I see them smacking against the dashboard as our party [I assumed he meant the killer] drives the car from the place of death. The noise bothers him. He takes the keys off the dangly thing [the chain] for this reason—to stop the other attachments from smacking against the dash as he drives along.

"The person driving the car is dark-haired and stockily

110

built . . . a young man . . . he's wearing bermudas, a short-sleeved shirt, and gym shoes. I see this person as you would see someone from across a parking lot at night . . . I see his body but I can't see his face. He drives onto the parking lot just as the store is closing [this would be 10:00 P.M. on Wednesday, June 12]. He can't bring the car back any sooner because there are too many people in the lot when the store is open . . . he can't do it any later because it would be too obvious being in that lot after the store is closed. So he comes at closing time. . . . His main reason for coming back is to get his own car, which he has left parked on the north side of the lot. He drives to the south side of the lot, where he knows that the employees of the store are told to park their cars. [After parking the victim's car] I sense this person searching his pockets and thinking, 'Have I got everything off me that might point me to it?' He is wearing the sunglasses as a disguise . . . there is a last-minute getting rid of the sunglasses . . . the keys are [also] thrown down on the floor. The party gets out of the car and checks himself again. 'Have I left anything behind?' he asks himself. He thinks not . . . but he has . . . the bermudas are frayed at the bottom and a string has fallen off and remains in the car [a brown string was found on the floor of the death car—this obscure fact of evidence was never published]. He pushes down the door-lock button and slams the door shut. He leaves a smudge of his palm print on the door [several unidentified smudges were found on the car door]. There may be other fingerprints in the car—were there? [I replied that some unidentified partial prints were found in the car.]

"The police have them, but they don't have them, eh? No matter, the person does not think of this at this time. He walks from the victim's car toward the store. The doors of the store are locked. He acts upset and disgusted about this . . . wants anyone who may be watching to think that he doesn't know the store has just closed . . . he says, 'Darn it, I'm just a couple of minutes too late.' He turns around and walks back to his own car on the north side of the lot . . . gets in it and drives home. . . . Perfect, nobody noticed him or what he was doing."

I asked Dodd to name the person who returned the death car or at least describe him more fully than he had. Dodd insisted that he could not do this. I returned to the subject of the keys, telling Dodd that only one key was found on the floor of the death car and that the second key was found sometime later in another place. "How did the second key get from the floor of the car to where it was eventually found?" I asked. (I did not tell Dodd that the second key was found on a hook in the garage where the car was being stored.) Dodd answered, "The people who opened the car had something to do with the second key not being found for some time. If I could just see or talk to these people I could tell exactly what happened. But by talking with these people I would only bring back the mistakes that the police made. . . . They will be very reluctant to let me talk to these people because the police don't want their mistakes brought up."

We talked for another hour, but Dodd could tell me only one more thing of any seeming import: he said that the piece of blue terry cloth found in the shopping bag on the back seat of the car was "not important . . . it was hers . . . she was trying to match the color" (when shopping for sewing material, I assumed him to mean).

In previous contacts Dodd had "sensed" what happened to Miss Butler up to the point of her being abducted from the parking lot. In the third contact he "sensed" how her car and body were returned to the lot. This was all very interesting, but the key issue was what happened to the victim between her abduction and the return of her body. Dodd was avoiding the heart of the matter and I wondered why.

My full-time assignment to the murder case ended after the second contact with Norman Dodd. Subsequent contacts with him were made on my "own time" and nothing was printed about them. However, word of the fact that I was contacting a clairvoyant in regard to the murder case spread about the *Daily News* and caused a considerable amount of comment. The reactions from my coworkers ranged from derision ("Has your spook chaser solved it yet?") to awe ("Boy, are you lucky to be working on something like this—I'm fascinated by ESP and can't wait to read your story").

Some of our nonnewspaper friends also became aware that I was contacting a clairvoyant in regard to the murder mystery. Linda Keagan, for one, was a frequent visitor in our apartment during this period and asked many questions about extrasensory perception. The widowed school-teacher said she did not believe in ESP; however, she talked about the subject at great length. And at times she was so persistent that it almost seemed to me that she was pumping me for information, especially my opinion of the alleged clairvoyant Norman Dodd. I feared that if she became convinced that he was genuine she would come up with a list of questions for me to put to Dodd about the fate of her late husband's soul; thankfully it never came to this. When I told her about Dodd's prediction that the unmarried reporter at the newspaper was pregnant, she surprised me by revealing a knowledge of her and by saying, "Good! I hope she is in trouble—the bitch made a play for my husband once."

I thought that the victim's parents might be interested in knowing what was going on. On Tuesday, August 13, I phoned Mrs. Bernard Butler and asked if she would talk with me.

"I don't know what good it would do," she replied. "My husband gets upset just knowing how upset I get talking about what happened. My husband and I have the feeling that it was all just an accident: they didn't mean to do what they did."

Shortly after 5:00 P.M. on Saturday, August 17, Dodd phoned me at my apartment and said in a very excited tone of voice, "I've come across something unbelievable—a man who has confessed the murder!"

I drove Dodd to the Kettering police station, where he told Lieutenant Horn this story:

"I had been in a milling sensation all day. I knew that something was going to happen. I called a woman I know and told her I sensed an incident she'd had with a man who'd exposed himself to her. She said, 'That's right.' We talked awhile and then she asked me what I had been doing lately. I answered, 'Working on a murder case.' She asked, 'Barbara Butler?' I said that she was right and then everything seemed to release in her. She said, 'I know a man who told me he did it.' "

Dodd identified the confessed killer of Barbara Butler as being "a man named Johnson [a pseudonym] . . . he works on the loading dock at a party-supply warehouse. But he likes to act like a big shot—tells everybody he's a

113

salesman. I've been told he's got a beer gut and a receding hairline," Dodd added. The woman, whom Dodd identified as Mrs. Florence Dunningham (a pseudonym), the wife of a prominent Kettering businessman, met Johnson, according to Dodd, "when he tried to sell her some supplies for a picnic. . . . She is the social chairman of a women's group—some kind of sorority—that was going to have a picnic. . . . Johnson wanted her business. . . . I sense that he also wanted Mrs. Dunningham, because he's the same fellow who exposed himself to her."

Still chuckling to myself over that remark, I left the police station with Dodd after Lieutenant Horn said that he would contact Mrs. Dunningham on Monday and ask her to verify Dodd's tale. On the way home, an incident occurred which was anything but funny. I had hay fever at the time and was sneezing intermittently as I drove with the clairvoyant along a back road toward Dodd's home. We were discussing the absence of strangulation marks over the throat and nape of the murder victim's neck when I sneezed and fumbled through my pants pocket for a paper handkerchief.

Dodd produced a cloth handkerchief from his own pocket and handed it to me, saying, "Use this."

"No, thanks."

"Please take it. I want you to have this cloth handkerchief."

"I've got plenty of paper ones . . . I don't want to dirty up your good cloth handkerchief."

"I have more just like this one. . . . You should always carry a cloth handkerchief with you . . . they can be useful for things other than wiping one's nose. The party we have been discussing found cloth handkerchiefs to be very useful."

On the afternoon of Monday, August 19, Lieutenant Horn informed me that he had located but had not talked to a man named Johnson. "I think he's the Johnson that Dodd told us about," Horn said. "He works nights on a loading dock." Johnson was twenty-nine years old and had a criminal record for minor offenses dating back to the mid-1950's. "He's the type who will quote us Miranda as we bring him in the door," Horn said, "so it won't do any good to pick him up unless I can tie him into the murder real good." Horn added that he had made an appointment to "see

Mrs. Dunningham tonight. If she backs up Dodd's story about this Johnson confessing the Butler thing, then we'll give him a real checking out."

Late that night I was awakened by a phone call from Dodd. "I went to see the woman tonight," Dodd said. "She told me that Lieutenant Horn had been to see her and she told him the same story she told me. The cop had an old picture of Johnson that he wanted Mrs. Dunningham to identify. She said the old picture was 'a great likeness' but she couldn't positively identify it as being the same Johnson who confessed."

"That's good," I mumbled, still only half awake.

"Then I went to the Ontario Store and walked around the parking lot. I had the same feeling I had before. . . . I felt that slap in the same place."

"Well good, Norm, that's fine."

"That's all right for you to say," Dodd snapped. "You didn't get slapped in the face like I did!"

On Tuesday, August 20, Lieutenant Horn informed me that "there's no way this guy Johnson's prints will match with the partials we found in the Volkswagen. Mrs. Dunningham confirms Dodd's story, though, so I'll continue to check on him."

Horn also said, "This Mrs. Dunningham is scared of Dodd. She told me she met Dodd after letting it be known that she wanted to see a fortuneteller. Dodd was suggested to her. She saw him only once, she says, but has talked to him on the phone several times. He didn't go see her last night; he called her up and tried to talk her into seeing him. She's got a sorority meeting Wednesday and Dodd doesn't want her to go—he wants her to see him instead. I advised Mrs. Dunningham not to see or talk to Dodd if she's as scared of him as she tells me she is."

On Thursday, August 22, Horn told me, "I've done all the checking behind this guy Johnson that I can do without picking him up. I've got nothing to tie him into it [the murder] at this point. I can't pick him up without putting Mrs. Dunningham and her family in danger of harassment. Johnson has a history of getting drunk and causing trouble. He must know by now that I've been checking on him. If he would call up and complain about it, then I've got a door open to talk with him. As it is, I'm in a bind and will just have to sit on it for a while."

Recent decisions of the United States Supreme Court have made the confession worthless to police as evidence unless the confession is made in the presence of an attorney or following the signing of a waiver of rights against self-incrimination. Johnson's brief appearance in the Butler case pointed out this fact and also told something of human nature. Lieutenant Horn told this story:

"One of the persons I checked with on Johnson was, of course, his employer. I had to tell the man why I was making my inquiry. When I had finished asking my questions about Johnson, the employer said:

" 'I want to find out as soon as possible about Johnson. If he's okay, I want to give him a raise because he's a good man on the docks; if he's involved in the murder case, I want to fire him!' "

17

On the evening of Friday, August 23, I was told that there was a second clairvoyant. The report was made to me in confidence by a Kettering detective—who had been assigned to the Butler case in its early stages, but then was taken off the investigation for some reason which was never explained. He said, "This guy Dodd isn't the only clairvoyant our people have working on the Butler case. They've got another one who, unknown to you, takes off on the Butler case about the same way your guy does." (Kettering police officials later flatly denied this, one of them saying, "Where did you hear a thing like that? If you got it from your clairvoyant, he's getting bad!")

I was mad. I phoned Dodd and told him what the Kettering detective had told me.

"What?" Dodd shouted. "It makes me look like a damned fool with somebody standing behind me looking over my shoulder."

"Exactly the way I feel. Norm, can you find out who this second clairvoyant is?"

"I'll find out. I'll put this out to my sources and call you back as soon as I hear."

"What was that?" Warning bells rang throughout my mind. There was a long pause.

Then Dodd said, "Matter of speech . . . I'll call you back as soon as I sense something."

On the morning of Saturday, August 24, Dodd called back to report: "I've got that other clairvoyant's name for you: it's Mrs. Marcella Walters [a pseudonym]. She's a spiritualist minister. She thinks she's a big shot. But she's not! Believe me, she's a phony."

"Did you find this out by ESP or by just doing some checking?" I asked.

"A little of each."

"How do you know she's a phony?"

"Because she told me one time that she was going to get her license."

"Her license?"

"Her fortunetelling license. I remember her saying to me, 'Honey, when you get the license you can get the money.' "

"You know this woman well?"

"Yes. I went to the spiritualist church for help after I found out I was this way. I was looking for a way to use my powers. Mrs. Walters is the minister of the church I went to. She's a minister of the church on Sundays and a manicurist the rest of the week . . . a real phony!"

"How do you know she's the other clairvoyant on the case? Did you ask her?"

"No! I called up one of the trustees of the Ohio Spiritualist Association and asked him. He told me even though he's a hanky-panky minister himself. He sells water softeners and cookware door-to-door weekdays and plays minister on Sundays."

I read too much into that remark to laugh at it. Dodd's slip of the tongue the night before combined with his revelation of spiritualist contacts made me feel sick to my stomach.

Dodd babbled on: "Those spiritualists offered me a church, but I said no . . . there are too many charlatans

117

in the spiritualist church and I'm not like that . . . I'm
not a charlatan!"

"You're not?"

"No! Wait, I'm getting something important."

"What's that?" I asked halfheartedly.

"I have a time lapse of a year. Was there a murder or
something in the Ontario Store lot about a year ago that
I am picking up?"

"A girl was robbed in that lot about a year ago. . . .
The person responsible for that attack was questioned in
the Butler case, but he cleared himself."

"Something that happened in the Ontario lot a year
ago is connected with Barbara's murder. I may have to
go into a trance to find out about this. . . . If I learn
anything, I will call you back."

18

I went to work at the Dayton *Daily News* on
the afternoon of Saturday, August 24, wondering if Dodd
had, in his anger over the report of a second clairvoyant,
inadvertently revealed himself to be something other than
a clairvoyant. Had all of the hours spent working with him
in the preceding weeks been in vain? He had told me of
"sources," spiritualist contacts, and an association with a
fortuneteller interested in the moneymaking possibilities of
her craft. Dodd himself had labeled these people charlatans.
What was Dodd? I was suspicious, but without a firm answer
to any of the many questions that crowded my thoughts.

I walked into the newsroom hoping that a busy, newsy
afternoon and evening on general assignment would help
me get my mind on a subject less confusing than that of
Norman Dodd. But for me, the biggest news of the day
was contained in a letter I found in my mailbox a few
minutes after arriving at the newspaper. The letter was
from Dr. J. B. Rhine and its subject matter was the alleged
clairvoyant abilities of Norman Dodd. Rhine was replying
to a letter I had written him on August 19, in which

I had informed the parapsychologist that Dodd had said of Rhine:

"He's very conscious of his feet. They are either bothering him or. . . . Does he have any trouble with his left ear? . . . He strokes his face."

In his reply, Rhine wrote that Dodd was correct on all three points. On the matter of the problem with his feet, Rhine said that no one—not even members of his family, to his knowledge—had known about it. He explained the problem as being a chronic condition which required daily care and was the only matter for which he had gone to a physician in fifteen years.

Rhine continued by saying that he indeed had trouble with his left ear, indicating it was a skin ailment that caused both pain and irregular bleeding.

The parapsychologist added that he had a tendency to stroke his face in what he considered to be an unusual manner. He said that he ran his hands across his forehead and then pressed them against his face in an attempt to rid himself of distractions while trying to express himself in difficult situations, such as at a conference or before a study group.

I read Rhine's letter in a mood of growing excitement. The man who had introduced the term "extrasensory perception" to the language was, I thought, telling me that Norman Dodd had been able correctly to "sense"—from a distance of hundreds of miles—obscure facts about Rhine himself. My earlier suspicions of Dodd the clairvoyant were swept away. I had, I thought, one hell of a good story. As a newspaperman, my first impulse was to rush to my typewriter. Rhine advised me to do no such thing. He said that although Dodd's ability looked very much like the real thing, the situation had to be handled cautiously and without publicity. He was a scientist who wanted more proof and suggested that the next step in an evaluation of Dodd's ability be a tryout of what he termed some simple tests.

The initial test, for which Rhine gave detailed instructions, would be an attempt by Dodd to match coded opaque envelopes, containing information on various types of police cases, with cards upon which the types of cases were identified.

Rhine said that it did not matter whether or not the types of cases used in the test were solved cases. He did say that the more definite the information on them is, the better. For definite information on police cases and for help in the making up and administering of the test, I needed the assistance of the Kettering police.

Kettering Police Chief John Shryock and Lieutenant Albert Horn were shown Rhine's letter. I then said, "The world's leading parapsychologist has told us Dodd may be the real thing and has given us advice on how to find out more about him and how he works. I think we ought to follow that advice and give Dodd the test."

Shryock, after saying, "I don't believe in this ESP—but we've got to try anything," agreed to cooperate. Lieutenant Horn would, he said, prepare the necessary test materials.

19

On the evening of Tuesday, August 27, Norman Dodd was taken to a room in the Kettering municipal building and presented with the following problem:

On the desk were five large cards bearing labels that identified them as being five different police cases: a "burglary of a school," a "robbery of a girl in a parking lot," an "armed robbery," a "homicide with a shotgun," and a "homicide of a girl in a parking lot." Next to the cards were twenty-five opaque envelopes containing information on, and articles relating to, the five cases. There were five identical sets of information for each case inside five separate envelopes. Each of the twenty-five envelopes, however, bore a different code number on the outside back of the envelope.

The five envelopes relating to the Butler case (the homicide of a girl in a parking lot) contained copies of her birth certificate, driver's license, a color portrait, social security card, and a synopsis of the case. Similar information was in the envelopes relating to the other four cases. (These cases were solved and the police thus had definitive answers for them.) The test materials were prepared and the envelopes coded by Kettering Police Lieutenant Horn, according to Dr. Rhine's instructions.

Dodd was asked to go through the stack of twenty-five envelopes—handle them, look at them or examine them in any way he chose short of opening them—and then attempt to match the information in the envelopes with the type of case they referred to (e.g., if he sensed that a particular envelope contained burglary information he was to place that envelope on the table on top of the card labeled burglary).

"You're playing truth or consequences with me," Dodd exclaimed, indicating that he both understood what he was being asked to do and did not like it. "This is the first time that I've tried to read blindfolded," he added.

It was 7:30 P.M. by the clock on the wall of the Kettering municipal office where the test was being conducted. Dodd seemed quite hesitant to proceed, avoiding the issue by saying such things as:

"On the way in here ⊿ noticed a Ford parked outside . . . do you own such a car by chance, Lieutenant Horn?" (Horn said that the Ford was his.)

"Downstairs in the police station . . . that street-light control box of yours . . . there's a short in your equipment—you may have a fire."

Dodd paced about the room examining the desks of city accounting department personnel. "Does a gray-haired woman sit here?" he asked Horn. Horn shook his head, indicating a no answer.

"Any of the suspects in the Butler case have a scar on his left elbow?"

Horn shrugged his shoulders.

We waited.

At approximately 7:45 P.M., Dodd returned to the desk containing the test materials, picked up several envelopes, ran his fingers over them, and then tossed them back on the table saying, "The man who prepared this test . . . his intention was to fool me . . . he did a good job. But the numbers three, five, and nine have been in my mind all day." He went through the stack of envelopes and pulled out the three envelopes bearing the code numbers 3, 5, and 9. "I set these aside as being the Butler case. . . . The card labeled 'homicide of a girl in a parking lot' is the Butler case, isn't it?"

He was told that it was.

"But I need two more envelopes for that, don't I? All

121

right, I will group envelopes three, five, nine, seventeen, and thirteen together as the Butler case."

"Take your time," Horn counseled. "There's no rush about this."

"You've made it easy for me by putting the same information in each of the five envelopes on a particular case. It's one hundred to one that I'll get them all right."

"I'm a generous guy," Horn said, with a wink.

Dodd's confident mood vanished as quickly as it had appeared. For five minutes he stood staring at the twenty as yet unmatched envelopes. Then he began to shuffle the stack. He seemed very depressed. "I'm doing this bass-ackwards," he mumbled.

"You've been on your feet ever since you've been in the room. Why don't you sit down for a minute and rest a bit?" Horn suggested.

"No!" Dodd snapped. "I can't sit down . . . if I did, I might pick up something from the person who sits in the chair during office hours here. . . . It would only confuse me."

Dodd then walked to the opposite side of the room from where Horn and I were sitting and began to lean against the municipal safe. At first he stood with his right elbow against the top of the safe, his head cradled in his right hand. Gradually he began to slump his body forward until, at length, the entire upper portion of his body was in contact with the broad top of the safe. He covered his head with his arms and then announced:

"Lieutenant, someone has been stealing money out of here! I suggest you investigate to find out who the thief is."

Horn whispered to me, "When this is all over, let's get adjoining beds at the same rest home!"

Some ten minutes later Dodd came out of another period of silence and inactivity by shouting this question at Horn: "Ever been to a séance?"

"No," the detective replied, "I can't say that I have."

"Would you go to one with me?"

"For what purpose?"

"I've just realized that there is one person who knows who the murderer is: the victim! Let's go to a séance . . . let's ask Barbara who did it!"

I grimaced. Horn's face was an expressionless mask. Neither of us said a word.

"I've got a strong impression of a goblet," Dodd said enthusiastically. "Goblets are used in séances. I must find the right goblet in order to conduct my séance."

"Ever conducted one of these séances before?" I asked.

"Yes! Two years ago, before I knew I was this way."

"Your parents," Horn asked. "Did they ever conduct séances or anything like that?"

"My father sensed things as a boy, but passed them off because of his father's strict Christian attitude. My mother knows that I have the power . . . I sense things that happened when she was carrying me. . . . We were in a cabin and tar leaked through the roof. . . . I mentioned this to my mother years later and she said, 'Yes!' "

With that, Dodd leaped up on a counter, looked down defiantly upon the detective and me, and said, "I've got to stand up here . . . I've got to be in a place where no one normally is in this room because I was picking up other people's thoughts down there on the floor."

I snickered. The detective stared up at Dodd.

"I know where I can conduct the séance!" Dodd shouted. "At Chesterfield, Indiana! The spiritualists from several states are encamped there now. They'll let me in if I come with a detective and a reporter!"

"Let you in?" I asked.

"Yes! I was refused admittance before because they said I had no background."

"A séance might be an idea for later on," the detective said, with his tongue figuratively well up in his cheek, "but right now, how about getting back to this little experiment we're conducting here tonight?"

Dodd appeared crushed. He jumped down from the counter, walked to the far side of the room, and then began to denounce spiritualists: "It wouldn't do any good to go to that camp . . . it's full of phonies. . . . Some of those charlatans make up to a million dollars a year off the suckers. . . . I know who they are—I can spot a phony before he can shake the table with his foot!"

The laughter that followed that remark seemed to relax Dodd. He then asked, "Would we believe Barbara even if she named the killer? Would she be able to name him? Would that be so illogical?"

"It is quite possible that the victim did not know her killer," Horn said.

At 8:45 P.M., Dodd finally began to make what ap-

123

peared to be a serious attempt to match up the twenty remaining envelopes with the cards identifying the four solved cases. As he did so he commented about things he sensed about these cases.

While working on the burglary case, Dodd said, "Two boys involved . . . one taller than the other." Lieutenant Horn said the two convicted burglars were both adults but that one of them was "heavier than the other."

Dodd took off on the "homicide with a shotgun" fairly well—correctly sensing that it occurred as the result of an argument and that the killer had "left to get a gun and come back." All of Dodd's comments on the "armed robbery" were erroneous. However, he acted quite sure of himself as he talked while matching up envelopes with the "robbery of a girl in a parking lot" card:

"This occurred a year ago in the same lot where the murder took place [this was correct]. The man who did it . . . something wrong with him upstairs . . . he acts peculiar . . . something about him that I can't put my finger on . . . a homosexual?"

"He's married," Horn replied.

"Funny . . . he's not very old . . . a young man." Horn nodded.

A few minutes after 9:30 Dodd had five opaque envelopes on top of each of the five label cards. Lieutenant Horn said that if Dodd wished to, he could go through the envelopes again or change any envelope that he felt uncertain of to another pile.

"I'll stick with beginner's luck," Dodd said; "always stick with your first hunch. Go ahead and score me; I want to know how I did."

I explained that Horn would determine how many correct match-ups Dodd had made by checking the five stacks of envelopes against his code (the key to which was locked up in his desk in the police station basement) but, I added, "We can't score you on this—I'll notify Dr. Rhine of how many you got right and he will have to tell us what your percentage means."

"Before we tally up, let's see if you get anything from looking at these," Lieutenant Horn said. He had spread twenty mug shots out on the top of a desk.

"What do you want me to do?" Dodd asked.

"Look at them and tell me whatever comes into your

124

head. . . . One of these is a photo of our friend Johnson . . . can you point him out to me?"

"Johnson? The man who confessed to Mrs. Dunningham? I've never seen him," Dodd protested.

"I was just curious to see if you could sense which one he is."

Dodd pointed a finger at one of the twenty photos and asked, "That him?"

"No."

Dodd pondered over the remaining nineteen mug shots for several minutes before asking, "Do you have the picture of a young subject here who was questioned in the Barbara Butler case?"

"Yes."

"He's the same man who robbed the girl in the lot a year ago."

"Right . . . and this is his picture right here. [Horn had removed a picture of Billy Joe Dean from among the other nineteen photos and handed it to Dodd to examine.] Can you tell me anything else about this fellow besides what you said earlier? You said there was something wrong with him upstairs, remember?"

"Yeassss." The word came out of Dodd's mouth in a syrupy, slurping sound.

Dodd examined the young man's picture for perhaps thirty seconds before concluding, "I don't think he's connected with Barbara as far as having done it. He was cleared of suspicion, was he not?"

"That's right."

"What happened to this bird Dean on the robbery conviction?" I asked.

"He got five years' probation and is back on the street."

Dodd returned to his search for Johnson. He studied the remaining pictures and discarded them one by one until he had reduced the pile to five. Then he reached in among the five remaining mug shots, picked out the photo of a young man and announced, "That's Mr. Johnson."

I looked to Horn for confirmation, but the detective's face was absolutely expressionless. "Why would you pick this picture as our friend Johnson?" Horn asked. "I remember you describing him as being potbellied with a receding hairline . . . but this picture is of a trim-looking young fellow with a full head of hair."

"Did I say that Johnson had a receding hairline?" Dodd

mumbled, obviously upset. "I was looking for an outgoing person and that's what I see in that picture. Well, let's try again. Is it this one?" he asked, holding up another picture.

"No . . . you were right the time before," Horn informed. "I just wanted to find out how convinced you were of your selection. . . . Too bad you forgot what you said earlier about sticking with your hunches."

Lieutenant Horn and I went to his desk in the detective section, got out the code, and learned that Dodd had made five correct match-ups out of a possible twenty-five.

He scored two right on the armed robbery and managed one correct match-up on the robbery, the shotgun homicide, and the Butler case; none of his match-ups on the burglary were correct.

His quick decision early in the test that the envelopes coded with numbers 3, 5, and 9 related to the Butler case was correct in only one instance—envelope number 3 contained Butler case information; 5 and 9 did not.

I didn't know how much ESP was indicated by a score of five out of twenty-five, but I needed no extrasensory powers to sense that Dodd was not all that he claimed to be. We left the police station at eleven o'clock on that late August night and I drove Dodd home, not a little bit apprehensive about all that he might be.

20

Dr. Rhine was informed of what I considered to be pertinent aspects of Dodd's behavior and statements during the test and was told the number of correct match-ups that Dodd had made.

The parapsychologist replied that a score of five correct out of twenty-five was, in his opinion, just chance. He indicated that ten or twelve correct would have been a good score and that even seven or eight correct match-ups would have been sufficient to warrant further experiments with Dodd. Ironically, Rhine implied that a score of zero, or only one or two correct, would have been more encouraging than Dodd's apparent guesswork score of five (an extremely low score might have indicated that Dodd had temporarily lost his ability due to nervousness or fear of the test).

I received the above information in a letter dated September 4, 1968. I notified the Kettering police and awaited further developments. In a subsequent communication, Rhine advised me to avoid further contacts with Dodd because it did not seem to him to be a game I could afford to play with the kind of man that Dodd now appeared to be. He reminded me that law enforcement was only incidental to my profession, and added that whatever the reason for the game Dodd was playing, he seemed pathological.

I decided to drop Dodd.

There was only one thing wrong with my decision.

Dodd decided that he would not drop me.

Three and a half weeks passed without incident. Then, on the afternoon of Monday, September 30, I looked in my mailbox at the *Daily News*, and found an envelope addressed: "Mr. Bill Clark, Daily News Staff Writer, Dayton, Ohio."

The *y* and the *t* in Dayton were not connected. I had seen that handwriting quirk before—in a chiding letter I had received just prior to my involvement with Dodd.

The envelope was postmarked: "Cincinnati, 29 Sep 1968."

I tore open the envelope, and was shocked to find a Christmas card inside.

The face of the card was a scroll, bordered with pine cones and green bows, and illuminated, in illustration, by the light beams of a lantern. The scroll was inscribed: "The charm of Christmas lies in the thought that we live in the memory of our friends."

I opened the card. This message, handwritten in ink, was on the left-hand inside page: "Dear Bill . . . if they found a old man's ring in the Volkswagon [*sic*], then check out the medic at WPAFB [an abbreviation commonly used in the Dayton area to mean Wright Patterson Air Force Base] who carrys [*sic*] Adhesive tape in his car all summer and lives off of women."

On the right-hand page was a printed wish for "A very Merry Christmas And all the Best Wishes for a Happy New Year."

127

The signature was a simple "Yours."

The *Y* in "Yours" was an unusual vertical scrawl that measured a full inch in height from the tip of the downward slant to the bottom of the looped stem. The other four letters of the signature were normally formed and only an eighth of an inch high.

I took the card and envelope to the Kettering police and had Lieutenant Horn check it for fingerprints. The sender of the card had been very careful: only several of my own prints came into view when a laboratory technician brushed away his magnetic filings. I asked Horn for an opinion.

"No ring was found in the Volkswagen," he said.

"That's not the point," I insisted. "I've been sent a Christmas card in September with a cryptic reference to the murder case on it. This is the work of a sadist!"

"It isn't the work of one of your true friends, that's for sure," Horn replied. "The person who sent you this may try to communicate with you through the mails again. Try to keep an eye out for anything with this unusual handwriting on it. If you can get it to us without opening the envelope, we can shoot it full of iodine and have a much better chance of lifting a print off the contents."

"What about Dodd?" I asked the detective. "What are you doing about him?"

"What can I do? He volunteered to help with this investigation. We went to him—he didn't come to us. All we know from that report you got back from Dr. Rhine is that Dodd isn't much as far as his ESP goes. You—as a private citizen and a newspaper reporter—can assume what you want to from that; but I'm a cop and I can't *prove* a damn thing by it!"

Sometime between eight and eight-thirty on the night of Tuesday, October 1, I answered the telephone in my apartment and heard Norman Dodd's voice purr, "I've been thinking about you."

"You have? Ah . . . in what way?"

"You need help . . . something has happened to upset you . . . you need advice."

"Oh? About what?"

Dodd paused and then changed the subject: "I was discouraged after that night when I took the test. . . . I sensed that I did not do well . . . I did not, did I?"

"Well, you were about average," I replied half truthfully.

"Hmmph . . . I must tell you that there are times when I can do this thing that I do and there are other times when it is boring to me. The test I took was boring . . . I could see no value in it."

"Uh-huh."

"Since then I have developed an entirely new concept with sensational results. I spent much of the weekend in Cincinnati working with an engineer on a silencer for jet aircraft. . . . A CIA agent is also interested in my services—they want me to locate a defector for them."

"Wait a minute! You were in Cincinnati on the twenty-ninth of September, were you?"

"What can I tell you, Bill?"

I told him about the Christmas card, figuring that his earlier jibberish was just his way of telling me that he had sent me the card. I described the card to Dodd and read him the message on it.

Then I asked, "What do you suppose it means?"

"The killer is trying to tell us something," he replied. "Maybe he's trying to give himself up around Christmas time."

"Why would he wait until Christmas? Why not right now?"

Dodd did not answer my questions. Instead, he said, "People who are mystic have a weird way of signing their names. I have a letter here in my hand . . . the person who wrote this letter did so with a peculiar flourish to the Y's."

"What are you trying to tell me, Norm?"

"These unusual flourishes . . . the Christmas card had them too, did it not?"

"It did. Does this mean anything to you?"

"The person who writes that way may be a jilted woman . . . someone who kept a close ear to the case. . . . Do you remember the lady who first sent the letter to the police?"

"Sure do . . . Mrs. Seckinger . . . what about her?"

"She has had a definite interest in this thing since the murder. I think she may have made the phone call to the newspaper saying that she knew something."

"Do you think that or do you know it?"

"I feel like going into a trance."

129

"Norm, what is this all about? I don't have time to play games."

"I have seen and talked of things that I do not understand. All the things that have happened are illogical . . . no pattern to them. I can tell you that it's the result of first-time luck—the killer has never done it before. I will leave you with these two thoughts:

"First, suppose that the killer's subconscious is planning another one around Christmas time. . . .

"Secondly, you are closer right now to nailing him than you've ever been in your life."

Dodd hung up.

The molestations began on the night of Wednesday, October 2.

My wife, Charlotte, and I were sitting in the living room of our apartment discussing my lack of success earlier that day in attempting to convince the police that they should do something about Norman Dodd.

"Bill, how can those stupid cops just shrug their shoulders after you told them what that crazy clairvoyant said to you last night?"

"They say that he's committed no crime and that they can't act unless he does. . . . They say the Miranda decision has put them in a bind."

"You know darn well that he's no clairvoyant!"

There was a moment of silence and then my wife and I heard three separate and distinct knocks upon the front door of our apartment. I stood up, ran to the door, opened it and . . .

"Honey," I yelled to my wife, "there's nobody here."

"You're kidding—there must be somebody there! I heard the knocks and you did too."

"Somebody knocked, all right . . . but whoever did it is long gone. I don't like this one bit."

I looked at my watch: it was 8:16 P.M.

I was working at the *Daily News* when, shortly after 11:00 A.M. on the morning of Thursday, October 3, my wife answered the telephone in our apartment and heard a voice say:

"Mrs. Clark? Ask your husband if he's done his Christmas shopping yet!"

The caller hung up. My wife did not recognize the

130

voice. She said that it was the voice of a boy . . . or a man with a not very masculine voice . . . or maybe someone disguising his own voice.

My wife and I were seated at our kitchen table having a late supper on the evening of Thursday, October 3, when we heard two separate and distinct knocks coming from the direction of the front door of our apartment. This time the knocks were followed by the sounds of running feet on the sidewalk outside.

"What time is it?" Charlotte asked.

"Eight-fifteen on the nose—same time as last night."

I went to the front door and opened it. No one was there.

I motioned to my wife to be quiet while I stepped outside and closed the front door behind me. I stood in the darkness with my back against the door and waited. All was quiet. Several minutes passed and then, from a hilltop about a hundred yards to the west, I heard:

"Fuck you!"

I would bet my life that the voice behind that curse belonged to Norman Dodd.

I informed officers on the Kettering police, the Dayton police and a detective in the Montgomery County sheriff's office (the latter had jurisdiction in the area where my family resided) of the October 3 incidents. The police attitude, in substance, was: "Well, what do you want us to do about it? Can you prove who was knocking on your door?"

I replied that, in my opinion, Dodd was not a clairvoyant but had made what sounded to me like a prediction that Barbara Butler's killer was planning another murder around Christmas time. The police informed me that there was nothing illegal about the making of predictions.

I knew then why so many people do not want to get involved. I had gotten involved in the Butler case because I wanted to help the police solve it, and only after they had asked me for assistance. The experiment with the alleged clairvoyant had failed. Now I was left to my own devices. One detective advised me, "If Dodd comes in your house—kill the bastard! If you do, just make sure that his body is inside your door when we get there."

My superiors at the Dayton *Daily News* were more sympathetic. They offered to either hire an armed guard to stand outside the door of our apartment or move my family to one of Dayton's southern suburbs—some fifteen miles away. My wife and I agreed that we could not live a normal life with a guard standing outside our door and that a move to another community in the Dayton area would not be any solution to the problem; if Dodd was involved and was determined to find us—he would be able to do so. We decided to give him every opportunity to make his move as soon as possible and get it over with; we turned down the offer of the guard and the move and, instead, I went to a gun shop and purchased an automatic pistol. I announced this fact to many of my friends and several of my coworkers at the newspaper.

Now we had a new bedtime ritual in our home. Each night before going to bed, my wife and I not only had to make sure the alarm clock was set—we also checked to be certain that the gun on the night stand was cocked.

The door knocking ceased, but my wife was subjected to a series of "breathing phone calls" at times when I was not at home. She eventually put a stop to this by telling the caller, "Keep breathing for three more minutes so the police can complete the trace on this call."

On Wednesday, October 9, *Daily News* medical writer Jayne Ellison arranged a meeting with two practicing psychiatrists—Drs. Joseph Trevino and D. A. Thomas—at which I told the doctors the story of my involvement with alleged clairvoyant Norman Dodd.

Dr. Trevino offered this opinion of Dodd:

"This person told you a lot at the start to make you think that he is genuine. He told you just enough, but not too much. If he is a compulsive psychopath, he may very well be trying to tell you he is and he's going to do something if you don't do something. If he is a paranoid schizophrenic, he can't come right out and say it—he feels that he can only give you hints that this is the case. I am very concerned about what might happen."

"Well, if he was involved," I said, "then that could explain how Dodd knew so many obscure facts about the murder and the victim. But, how do we explain how he knew the things he did about myself, my wife and Dr. Rhine?"

132

The question triggered a long exchange of opinions (directed at me) between the two doctors:

"If a so-called clairvoyant told me that my wife had tried on a particular pair of shoes the day before, I would have told him, 'Oh, so you're the one who's been following my wife around!' It's also possible that you told some friend about the picture in your wallet and that your friend somehow passed this along to Dodd—either intentionally or unintentionally. These are modern times—information gets around and people know people you don't think they know. Dodd told you that he had sources . . . and it's almost certain that your contact with him was very carefully set up. The statements that Dodd made about Dr. Rhine are harder to explain . . . but Rhine's a famous man and somebody could have written an article mentioning those things that Dodd told you about Rhine. If I was trying to palm myself off as a clairvoyant, I would read every word that I could about Rhine because he would be one of the persons I would expect to have to impress in order to be accepted as genuine."

The doctors said that Dodd was apparently a very unusual person and that they would like to talk to him. They insisted that I not call Dodd for this purpose. However, if Dodd should phone me in the future—the doctors advised me to regard such a possibility as a potentially significant action on his part—then I should attempt to interest Dodd in meeting with them. If such a possibility arose as a result of Dodd phoning me, the doctors suggested that I not tell him the exact nature of their professions. Rather I should tell him that I had discussed Dodd's work on the murder case with two scientists interested in ESP, and that these men had expressed an interest in talking with him. "If we can talk with this man for a couple of hours without his knowing exactly what we are," one of the doctors said, "we will be able to tell what he is."

21

A mild southern Ohio autumn gradually lengthened into winter without a word from Norman Dodd.

In October and early November I spent several days away from Dayton on assignment. My wife, although worried and apprehensive during these periods of my absence from home, was not molested by door knockings or phone calls. On November 26 she gave birth to our second daughter. My parents came from their home in upstate New York to care for our one-year-old while my wife was in the hospital and during her recuperation period. My father had recently retired, so my parents were free to stay with us indefinitely. They decided to remain through the holiday season.

The temperature went down and the Christmas decorations went up. I began to believe that the alleged clairvoyant had gone away and that his suggestion of death before Christmas was just a meaningless outburst from a sick and frightened mind.

On Tuesday, December 10, my wife and I were upstairs in our townhouse-type apartment putting the two babies to bed and my parents were relaxing downstairs when the phone rang at approximately 8:15 P.M. My father answered and heard a voice say, "Mr. Clark, may I speak to your son, please?" My father summoned me to the phone. I put the receiver to my ear and heard Norman Dodd's voice say:

"Mr. Clark, that was your father who answered, wasn't it?"

I was stunned. Dodd had caught me off guard. I let him play clairvoyant for several minutes while I collected my thoughts. Dodd said he sensed that my father was retired . . . that there was "something wrong" with my mother's leg (she had fallen that afternoon and bruised a knee) . . . that my parents "lived in the Northeast" and had been visiting us for several weeks. All of this was correct. I was convinced that Dodd did not have extrasensory perception. Then how did he know? Did he have the apartment "bugged"? The phone line tapped? Or had he been spending a great deal of time outside the apartment watching and listening? The answer, whatever it was, was not good.

I tried to hide my concern by acting very impressed at everything Dodd said. He babbled on, making predictions about the stock market and the length of a strike then in progress at the National Cash Register Company. Dodd forecast that the market would "drop after the new man [Richard Nixon] is inaugurated but will eventually go on a broad swing higher than now." (Stock prices did, in fact, drop continuously during the first years of the Nixon administration; in the "recession" of 1970 investors were still looking back longingly to the highs of December, 1968.) He said, "The NCR strike will be settled after Christmas and not before, as Jeane Dixon says." (The huge NCR facility is a vital cog in the Dayton economy and the strike was causing considerable concern and hardship in the area. Dodd claimed that he had heard Miss Dixon predict an early end to the strike when the well-known female seer was in Dayton for a promotional appearance. The strike was settled *before* Christmas.) He told me that he now thought that the "murderer is definitely a female—probably someone who works at NCR."

At the time, of course, I had no way of knowing the rightness or wrongness of Dodd's speculations. I only feared that his phone call was the contact the two psychiatrists had warned me about. I had to try to get Dodd to meet with the two doctors, so that they could examine him . . . trick him into it if need be by telling him two "scientists" were interested in talking with him about ESP.

Dodd ignored my first attempt to get the conversation on this trail, informing me, instead, that:

"The *Daily News* has a shortage problem in the area of a local column. You and I can solve this shortage. In place of the local columnist, who you will soon learn is resigning, the newspaper will have a new column . . . readers will write in and ask for a general analysis of their futures. . . . I will provide the information and you will write it."

"I don't know about that," I replied, "but I sure wish those two skeptics could hear you in action the way you are tonight."

"Skeptics? Who? Are they editors at the newspaper, perhaps?"

"No . . . just a couple of guys that I was talking to the

other day. . . . We got into a discussion of ESP and I mentioned all the tremendous things you did on the murder case, but . . ."

"They were not impressed."

"Well, they're scientists . . . they have to have things proved to them before they are willing to believe. I bet you could make believers out of them. . . . You sure have convinced me."

"Scientists, you say? I would be willing to talk to these men . . . but I don't know what I could prove to them if they are hardheaded about this."

"Oh, no, Norm . . . these men are very open-minded about the possibility of certain persons having ESP powers; they've just never had it demonstrated to them."

"If I meet with these men it will have to be on a week night and I would like some advance notice."

"Well, I'll have to check and see when they are available. But offhand I'd think that they would prefer a week night, too."

"As far as I am concerned, the weekends are out—I'm spending all of my weekends in Cincinnati working with some people on a very hush-hush project."

"You are, eh? That's interesting. Well, Norm, I'll give these men a call one of these days and try to set something up. Oh, one more thing—you said last fall that the murderer would strike again before Christmas. Do you still feel that way?"

"I had that feeling. Call me back as soon as you hear from those two scientists."

"It may be several days before I know."

"I must know as soon as possible. Good night, Mr. Clark."

The second that Dodd was off the line, I phoned Jayne Ellison and informed her that Dodd had made contact. We agreed that the two psychiatrists should be notified. She said she would phone Drs. Trevino and Thomas.

I asked Jayne if she could make any sense of Dodd's claim that the newspaper's columnist was resigning. She could indeed. The columnist had confided to Jayne that very afternoon that she planned to resign.

I was bewildered. "How can Dodd know of that?" I wondered aloud.

"Somebody could have told him," Jayne suggested. "Several people at the paper know she's quitting and they could have told any number of other people around town."

In early December my wife's mother had been called from her Connecticut home to Spokane, Washington, where her aged mother was hospitalized in critical condition. Her mother's condition stabilized, so on Thursday, December 12, my mother-in-law left Spokane and flew to Dayton to spend a few days at our apartment and see her new granddaughter.

There were now five adults and two children living in our small, five-room apartment.

Drs. Trevino and Thomas agreed to give Dodd an informal mental examination on the evening of Monday, December 16. The psychiatrists advised me not to tell Dodd the date of the meeting until at least Saturday, December 14, so as to give him as little time as possible to prepare for it by either "loading up" on information or doing something drastic to dramatize his alleged ESP abilities.

I was at work at the newspaper on the afternoon of Friday, December 13, when Mrs. Linda Keagan phoned my wife and invited herself to our apartment. Charlotte suggested that Mrs. Keagan postpone her visit "until after my mom leaves sometime next week. Things are pretty crowded in this little apartment right now with five adults and two babies all under one roof. Besides," Charlotte added, "that damned clairvoyant has come back at Bill again and we're all a little on edge." Mrs. Keagan said that she understood but that she was "coming over anyway."

Linda Keagan spent over three hours in our apartment that afternoon. Many matters were discussed.

Dodd called that night at his usual time—8:15 P.M. right on the dot—and really let me have it:

He knew that he was going to be asked to meet with two psychiatrists (not two "scientists" as I had told him) and could even describe one of them right down to his "Jewish nose" and "dark-rimmed glasses." He said that "someone very dear to your wife is there, but her mind is somewhere else—she is worried about somebody else in a hospital." (My wife's mother was visiting us, but her own hospitalized mother was, of course, very much on my mother-in-law's mind.) He asked, "Was there somebody at your apartment today complaining about a physical ailment?" I turned to my wife and repeated Dodd's question. Charlotte's jaw dropped. She was astonished but able to reply that Linda

Keagan had done a considerable amount of talking that afternoon about a physical ailment that had been bothering her.

Then Dodd demanded to know, "When am I going to be asked to perform mental gymnastics for those two doctors? When is the meeting?" I could see no point in lying to Dodd; he seemed to know everything anyway and I thought that my job was to get him in the same room with the two psychiatrists, not to be evasive and perhaps provide him with an excuse to refuse to see the doctors.

"Can you meet us at the newspaper Monday night about seven-thirty?" I asked.

"This coming Monday—the sixteenth?"

"Yes, if that's okay with you."

"Monday will be fine. I want to get this over with . . . it's getting pretty close to Christmas and we will all be wanting to spend as much time as we can with our families."

22

The alleged clairvoyant, Norman Dodd; two psychiatrists, Dr. Joseph Trevino and Dr. D. A. Thomas; two reporters, Jayne Ellison and myself, sat down around a table in the Dayton *Daily News* conference room shortly after 7:30 P.M. on Monday, December 16, 1968. The atmosphere was one of relaxed informality and the conversation, at first, was casual (it reminded me of typical after-dinner table talk among old friends). The mood began to change, however, shortly after Dr. Trevino smiled across the table at Dodd and said, "We understand that you've had some ESP experiences—would you like to tell us about them?"

Dodd, appearing quite sure of himself, began to talk. Jayne switched on a tape recorder. I started taking notes.

The psychiatrists listened as Dodd gave a rambling history of his psychic experiences. He said that many of these experiences "scared me, so I went to a spiritualist to be enlightened." Next, Dodd claimed, he "went to see Mrs. Grant [Mrs. Hester Jones Grant—the other clairvoyant suggested to me on August 1 by Mrs. Alice Seckinger], who taught me that there is a right way and a wrong way to meditate. From that point on, it has been an endless chain of people and events. Recently I have been able to see a number of disasters: an earthquake last week . . . a tidal wave that hit the east coast . . . a fire in Virginia."

The psychiatrists began to probe Dodd, gradually backing him into a corner with a series of leading, but gently posed, questions:

Q. These flashes of things that pass through your mind—do they happen before the incidents take place or afterward?

A. Usually before . . . two weeks to a few days before.

Q. Is this a sort of premonition that you get . . . something that just happens . . . or do you have to meditate on the subject in order to get an inkling of things that are going to happen?

A. A meditation is just something to relax. . . . As I said before, there is a right way and a wrong way to meditate.

Q. Straighten us out on that—what is the right way to meditate?

A. The wrong way is the act of talking out in the open where there are a great many people . . . traffic . . . vibrations. The proper way is by yourself . . . sitting or in a relaxed position.

Q. Isn't this just plain ordinary horse sense?

A. It may be to you . . .

Q. These premonitions or whatever you prefer to call them —you wouldn't call them visions because you don't really see these things, do you?

A. I see them happening mentally.

Q. How vivid are your pictures of these events? Can you actually visualize them happening or are they just incidents or blurs?

A. It's as vivid as if I was looking right at it—sometimes with color, sometimes without.

Q. When this happens . . . what does this do to you as a person? How does it make you feel?

A. Tired. (There was a pause.)

Q. What other reaction do you have?

A. I feel satisfied . . . exhausted . . . my energy has been expelled.

Q. Satisfied?

A. Satisfied!

Q. Now let me ask you this: you have had premonitions of terrible events—is that right?

A. Yes.

Q. And they subsequently happen—these terrible events in which people lose their lives, I mean?

A. Yes . . . other people can verify this. . . . My wife reads the Cincinnati newspaper . . . I, of course, do not read newspapers.

Dodd chattered on for several minutes trying to explain himself; then an expression of concern spread across his face and he fell silent, perhaps realizing, a minute too late, the trap that the psychiatrists had helped him talk himself into.

"How can this be satisfying to you?" Dr. Trevino asked. "How can you justify being satisfied at experiencing a tragedy which you say you know is going to happen and cause a considerable loss of life?"

Dodd appeared shaken; he mumbled his reply: "The tragedies are something that I cannot change. . . . They are satisfying only in the knowing that they are going to happen. . . . I never worry about what I see . . . I just say, 'Let that pass.' "

The psychiatrists informed Dodd that he could not let a vision of a frightening occurrence "pass" without some type of response. "There's something missing here," Dr. Trevino explained. "We human beings respond to stimuli . . . and the stimuli that you have experienced—your visions of frightening happenings—produce impulses . . . you have to respond to them. . . . If you are a sadist, you may respond by being glad . . . or you may be frightened or confused . . . but there has to be a response—some type of feeling."

"I never looked at it like this," Dodd said in a voice that was almost a whine. "If I stopped and pondered over these things, I would be frightened."

Dr. Thomas asked, "If you stopped and pondered over it, would you have any feeling of wanting to prevent a frightening experience from actually occurring?"

Dodd replied that he would, but was evasive when asked to explain what he would do to prevent such an occurrence. He began to talk about Barbara Butler's murder. He would mention a point he had made to me back in August, look at me, and ask, "Isn't that right, Bill? Didn't I say that?" Dodd produced no new information at this time, but his rehashing of the old appeared to help him regain a measure of his earlier confidence; he had, in effect, taken a breather.

About 8:30 P.M., Dodd stared first at Dr. Trevino and then at Dr. Thomas as he asked, "Do either of you gentlemen have a patient who at any time this past week expressed great pain?"

Dr. Trevino responded, "We get these every day. . . . It depends on what you mean by pain—mental? physical?"

"Physical!" Dodd shouted.

The two psychiatrists shook their heads negatively.

"Look for it . . . you will! I can't tell you when . . . I can tell you that it will be a female."

Oh, my God, I thought to myself, is Dodd trying to tell us another girl will die? Is he trying to tell us one is dead right now?

There was a long pause, during which Dodd pressed the palm of his right hand against his forehead as if he was in deep thought. Then he whispered, "It will be her back."

Jayne Ellison moistened her lips.

I felt my heart in my throat.

The doctors stared across the table at Dodd and Dodd stared back at them. Then Dodd asked, "Do either of you gentlemen have a daughter?"

Dr. Trevino answered, "No."

Dodd put his hand to his forehead again and mumbled, "There is a girl in trouble . . . I don't know what it is."

There was another period of silence, which was broken by this question from Dr. Thomas: "This person in pain . . . first you said 'had pain,' then you said 'will have pain.' Which?"

"If you haven't," Dodd replied, "you will know of this in the very near future."

"Is it occurring or is it going to occur?" Dr. Thomas asked.

"Occurring," Dodd whispered, "it's occurring."

For nearly a minute the only sounds in the room were those of labored breathing. Then the psychiatrists peppered Dodd with questions, searching for another weak spot:

Q. What do you do?

A. I love God.

Q. Would you call yourself a religious person, then?

A. I thought once that I would be a Catholic priest . . . but I changed my mind when I realized that all religions are man-made and fakes. . . . Certain parts of religion satisfy my soul. I don't smoke, drink, gamble, or carouse around with strange women. . . . Smoking is a vice, a crutch, a sign of insecurity.

Q. Is your work satisfying to you?

A. Yes . . . it leaves me free to choose responsibilities, and to work at these responsibilities until I achieve satisfaction.

Q. Do you do any methodical type of work?

A. Yes.

Q. These flashes, or premonitions, that you have—do they occur during working hours even when there are other stimuli around?

A. Yes!

Q. Noises don't bother you, then?

A. There are times when they do.

Q. But there are times when, no matter what the noise process is, you still can create what we call a trance?

A. Yes. I am able to hypnotize myself . . . I learned hypnotism after becoming interested in it as a boy in high school.

Q. These so-called hypnotic trances of yours—do you feel tired afterward?

A. Yes.

Q. How tired?

A. Drained.

Q. Perhaps we misunderstood you earlier. . . . Didn't you say at the beginning that these flashes or trances happened just like that [snap] without your having to do anything to create them?

A. Yes.

Q. But now you say you do have to create them at times?

A. Yes.

Q. Can you recall anything else that you did not recall before?

A. I don't feel that your reasoning is accurate . . . I feel you are trying to say that it's me doing it.

Q. Is the murderer from Dayton?

A. Yes.

There was a moment of silence, and then, enunciating each syllable of the phrase in a deep tone of voice, Dr. Thomas said:

"Fingerprints on the car."

Dodd began to giggle.

142

I scratched my head, trying to recall if I had ever seen this man laugh before.

The psychiatrists and Jayne Ellison glared quizzically at Dodd.

He offered this muttered explanation: "I'm laughing because . . . these people . . . the local politicians . . . in a . . . ah, a small community like Kettering . . . ah, I would hate to work under those circumstances where this political boundary is set up. . . . I'm not saying it's political . . . I'm saying that the police are lax . . . not nearly as efficient as they should be. . . . If anyone has a job to do, he damn well should do it . . . regardless. . . . I don't care what your job is—if you do it, you should do it . . . with as good intentions as anything else you do."

Dr. Thomas asked, "Why did fingerprints trigger this?"

"Because I told them where fingerprints were found on the car! Didn't I, Bill? I told that the fingerprints were found where they slammed the door! And the police said, 'Well, yeah, er, ah . . .' "

"They fumbled!" Dr. Thomas exclaimed.

"It was distracting," Dodd responded, "because you couldn't get a straight answer from these people. . . . It was yes, no, indifferent . . . and if they did have any feelings they would conceal it."

"What does this make you think of?" Dr. Trevino asked.

"It makes me disgusted!"

Trevino inquired, "Do you feel they didn't want to answer?"

"They just couldn't answer," Dodd snapped. "They didn't check!"

The psychiatrists attempted to seize upon Dodd's obvious anger. "In other words," Dr. Thomas said, "the clues were there but the damned police didn't pick them up!"

In his response Dodd sought other targets for his passion: "Dayton is one of the biggest credit card towns that ever lived . . . the people are being led. . . . For instance: we put a great deal of responsibility, money, and time into public services such as the police department . . . but yet every time there is a homicide, we immediately rush all our evidence to the FBI when we have a quarter of a million dollars of technical equipment right here. . . . It's ridiculous!"

Dodd was attempting to escape—to channel his anger away from the murder case and thus compose himself; but

Dr. Thomas figuratively reached out and pulled him back into the murder by saying, "I think the word *fingerprints* is a key here . . . it's a prime factor since it's triggered off the outburst."

"It was," Dodd admitted. "I told them where these prints were. . . . My feeling was: how could you have missed them because they were so clear to me? On the mirror . . . on the side of the car . . . and the seat handle . . . places where you would normally look for fingerprints, but they missed them!"

Dodd paused a moment, then directed himself to the doctors. "If I gave you an answer . . . and you said, 'Okay, thank you' . . . and you put it in your pocket, filed it away, and then said, 'What else?' what would that make me feel about you?"

"That I was not interested," Dr. Trevino replied.

"All right!" Dodd exclaimed, and then launched himself into a lengthy tirade against the victim's parents, claiming, among other things, that they were not as concerned about the solution of the case as he would have been in similar circumstances.

Dr. Thomas stated this assumption: "I get the feeling that what you're saying is: 'Damn it, the individual left the trail, why don't you take it? I left everything so you could catch, and you didn't catch!' I think this is what upset you, is it not?"

Dodd did not answer, but his will and self-control appeared to fade away and he became more and more responsive to the doctor's suggestions.

First he repeated, almost word for word, the story he had told me in August about the return of Miss Butler's Volkswagen and body to the Ontario Store parking lot. He acted everything out: checking the pockets of his blue suit while saying that the killer checked the pockets of his bermuda shorts; he made a leisurely tossing motion with his right arm while saying that the killer tossed the car keys and sunglasses onto the blanket-covered body. He described the killer in the same terms I had heard him use before: "young, dark-haired, heavy-set."

There was a brief pause, followed by this exchange of questions and answers:

Q. Any premonitions or flashes that this same person could do this again?

A. We got into this. . . . I believe the person could do it

144

again under the right set of circumstances . . . but by their-self, I don't think so.

Q. More than one person did this?

A. No! (The reply was a low-pitched moan.)

A. This is a particular person that we're talking about, or several persons?

A. Not persons . . . a person.

Q. An isolated rerun with the help of somebody else?

A. Possibly they kept in touch because they had such a success with the first one.

Q. But you have the feeling that it was done by one person?

A. Yes.

Q. Would this person take advantage of the confusion of the Christmas season—when no one pays too much attention to what is going on around them—to do this again?

A. There would have to be a relationship being dissolved . . . a breaking off . . . rejection. . . .

Dodd leaned forward in his chair until his head and shoulders were over the edge of the table in front of him. "I have a place," he mumbled. He brought his right hand up to the side of his face, snapped his fingers, dropped his right arm into his lap alongside his left, bowed his head, and said:

"Something snapped! I have a feeling of being caught . . . being found out . . . footsteps approaching. I saw a garage . . . sliding-type doors . . . possibly two."

The psychiatrists zeroed in on Dodd, pounding at him with their questions.

Q. What about the garage? How do you know about it?

A. I saw it . . . you made me volunteer the trigger.

Q. What part does the garage play in this?

A. The garage is a place to hide . . . a place to hide the body until the store closes.

Q. Where is the garage?

A. In that neighborhood . . . not far from the store.

Q. How do you know that?

A. Because of . . . the mileage . . . gas . . . car wasn't driven very far.

Q. What color is the garage?

A. White.

Q. A wooden garage?

A. Wood . . . it goes with a two-story house in front of it. . . . To the side of it is an apartment building with individual aluminum doors. . . . To the back of it there's an

145

alley . . . a wide alley. . . . Next to the alley there's [another] garage newly built out of cement block—this is also an apartment-type thing.

Q. Did the struggle happen in the garage?

A. The struggle happened . . .

Q. Where? Visualize it!

A. Not in the garage . . . somewhere else . . . then the car was brought back to the garage. . . . I went to the garage . . . saw the right-hand side of it being opened. . . . The car is inside the garage. . . . I see the beams of the garage— brown, very dry. . . . I see the clothes coming off in the garage.

Q. Visualize the struggle!

A. This relationship—they're narrowing it down!

Q. Tell us about the struggle: this we need to know!

A. The party who plays this part . . . the party is a man . . . I see it through this party's eyes . . . when I go behind the party to see—I have the short-sleeved sweatshirt.

Q. Sweatshirt?

A. Yes . . . the sweatshirt. . . . The basic struggle was over the clothes coming off her body. . . . This was the greatest struggle . . . unconsciousness occurred.

Q. How does she become unconscious?

A. Pardon me?

Q. What do we hit her with?

A. The fist! (Dodd screamed, slamming his right fist down upon the top of the table.)

I gagged. After all these months of searching for Barbara Butler's killer, I thought that now, here in this very room, I was watching a re-creation of her death agony.

Q. Why?

A. The first time was to make her obey . . . to make her leave the parking lot.

Q. Why do we hit her again?

A. To make her submit.

Q. How do we approach her? Do we know her?

A. This party came up to her casually . . . helped her put her packages into her car. . . . She's struck. . . . The party got into the car . . . and then . . .

Q. *Visualize it!*

A. I seem to see Barbara driving . . . the party is sitting in the car with her.

Q. What's the party's name?

146

A. No name called . . .

Q. You must tell us the party's name!

A. I don't want to finger anybody.

Q. Without this we have nothing. . . . Give us a name!

A. What name? I can't see it.

Q. Concentrate!

A. No name.

Q. What can you perceive, then?

A. I feel it was a fumbling accident that the killer got loose. . . . The killer is still at large merely because of fumbling by the police department. . . . The killing just happened. . . . Everything he did to make them fumble was planned after the killing. . . .

Dodd raised his head, blinked, and then let his eyes roam about the room. "Where have I been?" he asked. When no one replied to this, he said, "I have said things. The more I think about it the more I know it fits. I feel warm, nice!"

"It's getting late," Dr. Trevino said with a sigh. "I think we've gone as far with this as we can go tonight. If you'd like to try this again, Mr. Dodd, you just let us know when."

Dodd stood up, nodded to me, put on his overcoat, and walked out the door.

The doctors said they could not make an immediate diagnosis; they said they would have to "think over" Dodd's remarks and actions before attempting to render an opinion of him.

I went home and, in utter anguish, told my wife my opinion: "Another girl's been murdered! I know it! And there's not a God-damned thing that I can do about it!"

Charlotte suggested, "You can tell the police."

"Yeah, sure. I can tell the police that Dodd said a girl is in great physical pain. . . . I know what he meant by that, but what do I tell the police when they ask me, 'Where's the body?'"

23

Tuesday, December 17, was an all-day nightmare.

In the morning I went to work and attempted, without success, to concentrate on routine assignments. I did not *know* that a girl had been murdered, but I was so afraid that I did "know" that I found it impossible to think or talk of anything else. I told a number of people of my suspicions.

In the afternoon I *knew,* but I didn't have any proof of what I knew. At 1:45 P.M., the Kettering police announced that Regina Ann Duchnowski, twelve, of 1939 Farmside Drive, Kettering, had been missing for twenty-two hours and was now presumed to have been kidnapped. The victim was described as a slim, frail girl, who had been wearing slacks and a sweatshirt when last seen.

The news caused me to become quite emotional. "Sweatshirt!" I screamed. "That crazy clairvoyant claimed last night that he saw a sweatshirt being taken off Barbara Butler. . . . Butler wasn't wearing a sweatshirt the day she died!

"This missing girl hasn't just been kidnapped—she's been murdered! And for no reason!"

Then, in like measure, I cursed myself, the police, and the American system of justice for having been unable to prevent an innocent little girl from having to suffer, as Dodd himself had put it, "great pain."

The Kettering police notified the Federal Bureau of Investigation and its agents entered the Duchnowski kidnapping case Tuesday afternoon on the possibility that the victim might have been transported across state lines (the Indiana border is only some thirty miles west of Dayton and the Kentucky line is fifty miles to the south).

Police and volunteers searched the Kettering area without success.

It was a clear, brisk day. The ground was free of snow, but a fall of several inches was predicted in the overnight forecast.

Two Kettering residents, Gregory Crum and his girl-friend, Kyle Knight, had taken advantage of the existing weather conditions and gone for a horseback ride.

About 5:00 P.M. Crum and his companion were pro-ceeding homeward in gathering darkness along a trail through a wooded area in the Beavercreek Township section of Greene County. The two riders were less than a mile to the east of the Kettering city limits (which also serves as the Montgomery-Greene county line) and about four hundred feet inside the woods when Crum "saw something white." He dismounted, walked a few feet off the trail, and discov-ered the battered, seminude body of a young girl lying on its back among the branches of a fallen tree.

Crum notified the Beavercreek Township police of his find, which he said was so horrible that he would not permit Miss Knight to look closely at it.

The thicketed woods were shrouded in darkness and thus were virtually impenetrable when Chief Max LeVeck and other Beavercreek officers reached the area. However, the owner of the property, a man named Fred Pier, was able to guide the officers through the woods to the death scene. Pier also had some potentially valuable information:

He said that he had attempted to stop the driver of a tan Pontiac from leaving the area on a lane to the west of the woods about five o'clock the preceding (Monday) after-noon. He said that the driver of the car, whom he described as being a "young, dark-haired man," had ignored his order to stop and explain why he was trespassing. The car swerved around him, sped off toward a highway at the end of the lane, Pier said, and disappeared.

Word of the horseback riders' discovery spread rapidly throughout the Dayton metropolitan area.

The Greene County Sheriff's Department (headquartered in the county seat, Xenia, some ten miles east of the woods) and the Kettering police dispatched officers to the scene. The sheriff's deputies, according to Township Chief LeVeck, be-gan "trampling around all over and interrupting my investi-gation." In protest, LeVeck and his men "pulled out."

Greene County Sheriff Russell Bradley, a folksy person-ality but an experienced, capable lawman, reached the scene and took charge. He inspected the body: it was nude from the waist up (body clothing included a pair of white underpants, socks, and a pair of slacks pulled down about the ankles) and bore numerous signs of violence—among

149

them what appeared to be a severe injury to the back and discontinuous marks on the neck. Bradley stated the obvious —"the girl died a violent death"—and asked the Ohio Bureau of Criminal Investigation (BCI) for assistance. Then the sheriff ordered the woods to be sealed off and the body left as it was found pending the arrival of the BCI's mobile crime laboratory.

Illuminated by spotlights, the body lay in the woods, undisturbed and unidentified, for many hours.

Less than two miles west of the woods, a small white house at 1939 Farmside Drive in Kettering was decorated with symbols of cheer and religious conviction. There was a large Santa Claus on the front door and a madonna on top of the piano in the living room. But in the hearts of Stanley and Ann Duchnowski, the owners of the two-story Cape Cod-style home, there was agony and growing despair.

The Duchnowskis had learned from a television newscast that the body of a small girl had been found in Greene County.

"You'd think we'd have been informed about it by someone before it was put on the air," the mother said.

"Maybe not hearing about an identification is good news," a neighbor said in an attempt to buoy up the parents' sinking hopes that their twelve-year-old daughter would be found alive.

Stanley ("Ski") Duchnowski, a forty-eight-year-old unemployed bricklayer, sat in the kitchen listening to radio newscasts, smoking cigarettes, and drinking coffee. A visitor saw the father bury his head in his hands and then heard him wistfully recall that Regina "used to pick out a tune on the piano."

Four nuns, among them the missing girl's school principal and her sixth-grade teacher, attempted to comfort Ann Duchnowski. The mother frequently fingered her rosary beads and occasionally sipped a sedative prescribed by the family doctor. "I've cried till I can't cry any more," she said.

The younger Duchnowski children—John, six, and Mary Beth, four—were being cared for by neighbors. Their son Mike, seventeen, maintained a lonely vigil in an upstairs bedroom. A married daughter, Pam, twenty, was summoned home from San Francisco.

Hansel, Regina's pet dog, snooped about the house. "Oh,

how she loved that dog," a neighbor said. "The dog ran away one time and Gina cried and stayed awake all night over it."

At 1934 Farmside Drive, Mrs. Lewis G. Hart and her eleven-year-old son Tim revealed the circumstances of twelve-year-old Regina Duchnowski's abduction. The boy, in fact, had been an eyewitness to it.

Mrs. Hart said that Regina had come home from school the preceding afternoon (Monday, December 16), watered and fed her dog, done some homework, and then told her mother that she was going out to visit a friend.

Tim Hart had been kept home from school on Monday to recuperate from an attack of influenza. The boy said that he looked out his bedroom window about 3:30 P.M. and saw Regina "motion with her hands" as if she was giving directions to the driver of a car parked at the curb in front of the Duchnowski home. Tim said that he could tell from his vantage point across the street that "There was this man in the car and Gina—we all called her Gina—was talking to him. I couldn't see him too well . . . but it seemed like he had shaggy hair in the back . . . had on some sort of brown jacket . . . and didn't look like an old man to me."

The boy described the suspected kidnap car as being "an icky-colored Pontiac—it was bronze or tannish with sparkles in it . . . with white sidewall tires."

The man and the frail, bespectacled Duchnowski girl "talked for just a little time," Tim recalled, and then: "Gina walked around in front of the car . . . the man reached over and unlocked the door on the passenger side . . . she opened the latch and got in with him . . . he pulled out then, kind of slow, and drove off. . . . I ran downstairs and told my mother: 'Gina got into a car with a man. . . . I've got the license number and I'm going to keep it.'"

Mrs. Hart explained, "I honestly didn't think too much about it. I thought it might have been one of her brother's friends or something. . . . Then, later in the evening, Ann [Duchnowski] called me and said she was worried about Gina . . . that she hadn't heard from her and that they had looked everywhere. . . . I told her, 'Ann, I hate to say this . . . it gives me goose bumps . . . but Tim saw Gina getting into a car with a strange man this afternoon.' Well, Ann began to get real worried and then she called the police right away."

Kettering Police Chief John Shryock said that the Duchnowski case "at first appeared to be routine, but as time went on we became more concerned. We have many missing child reports each year, and 99 percent of the time the youngsters are found right away."

Tuesday evening two separate investigations were in progress: the Kettering police, with the assistance of FBI agents, were seeking the person who had apparently kidnapped Regina Duchnowski; the Greene County Sheriff's Department, with the help of Ohio BCI investigators, was seeking the person who had apparently murdered the unidentified young girl. (Police and sheriffs both implied later that each was kept in the dark about progress made by the other.) Both agencies, of course, had as their prime suspect the driver of a tan Pontiac. The sheriffs had a composite sketch of the driver drawn from information provided by Fred Pier; the police had a somewhat different drawing prepared from a description provided by young Tim Hart. Both drawings were of a male Caucasian with dark, curly hair and thick eyebrows; however, the sheriffs' sketch depicted an older, fuller-faced suspect than did the Kettering drawing.

The Kettering investigation received a seemingly shattering blow when it was determined that the neighbor boy's recollection of the abductor's license number—1968 Ohio registration number 88117 NN—was inaccurate. Acting on the possibility that 88117 NN was either a scrambled or a reasonably close version of the correct number, police began checking the ownership and make of vehicle of all Ohio auto registrations containing any combination of the numbers and letters 88117 NN.

It was a herculean task. Literally thousands of license numbers had to be examined because police could not be certain that the make of the suspected kidnap car was a Pontiac; they also had to take into account the possibilities that the license plates were stolen or registered in a name other than that of the suspected male abductor. Ohio license number 8771 NN was, in fact, one of the few combinations within the range of possibilities that police could discard with the absolute conviction that the registrant had no part in Regina Duchnowski's disappearance. Registration number 8771 NN was listed as a 1967 Volkswagen registered to Miss Barbara Ann Butler.

152

I informed Lieutenant Horn of the Kettering police, Detective Les King of the Montgomery County Sheriff's Department, and Greene County Sheriff Bradley of Norman Dodd's "girl in pain" statement. Then I called Dodd to find out what he had to say.

I began by asking Dodd if he had heard the news. "What news?" he responded. Then he reminded me that he did not read newspapers or listen to newscasts.

I told Dodd that a young girl's body had been found in Greene County. "Oh," Dodd began, in an almost unbelievably calm reaction, "I wonder if this is the female that I was telling you and the doctors about last night?"

I replied that I felt certain that it was.

Dodd quizzed me about his examination: "What did the doctors think of me?" "Was every word I said put down on tape?" "Did you have a transcription of that tape recording made for the police?" "That garage I described—have you found it yet?"

I answered, "The doctors haven't expressed any opinion yet . . . the whole session was taped . . . I had a transcription made . . . the police have been told of some of the things you said . . . I haven't found the garage—there are a lot of white, wooden garages in the Dayton area."

Then I said, "This girl was apparently kidnapped in a tan Pontiac . . . that's something like a brown Oldsmobile, isn't it?"

Dodd's response was to describe his car (which was quite different from either a tan Pontiac or a brown Oldsmobile).

After a pause he inquired, "If I went out there to the murder scene, do you think the police would let me take an infrared picture of it?"

Before phoning Dodd, I had thought that there was nothing further that this strange man could do or say to shock me. I had been wrong. I was quite upset by his revelation that he possessed infrared equipment. Did this mean that he was able to stand outside my apartment and take pictures through the drawn curtains or perhaps even the very walls?

I asked Dodd, "What purpose would there be in taking an infrared picture of the death scene?"

"There's a possibility," Dodd claimed, "that heat waves left by the killer will show up as an image of him on the film."

At a school construction site just to the east of the woods a group of newsmen stood huddled together, attempting to

153

ward off some of the ill effects of a cold, raw wind as they waited for information. It was 9:30 P.M. and, although more than four hours had passed since the discovery of the body, it had not yet been brought out nor had a positive identification been announced.

Emergency vehicles ringed the area—their headlights and spotlights probing at the inky blackness of the interior of the woods where investigators were searching frantically through the underbrush for evidence against a deadline imposed by an approaching snowstorm.

Stirred by the wind and illuminated by the lights, a thousand barren branches of a hundred scraggly trees appeared to dance about the fringes of the small forest. I thought of it as an eerie, haunting scene made even more disturbing to me personally by the presence at my side of Norman Dodd

Dodd had brought his infrared equipment and was constantly pestering me to obtain permission for him to enter the woods and photograph the death scene. I did not know whether there was a purpose behind Dodd's ridiculous scheme or whether it was simply another aspect of his lunacy. I did know that there was not one chance in a trillion of any of the killer's "heat waves" being present in the frigid woods twenty-four or more hours after he had left the scene. I told Dodd that I would inform Sheriff Bradley of his offer to film the scene.

Shortly before 10:00 P.M. Bradley emerged from the woods and confirmed that the victim was, indeed, Regina Ann Duchnowski.

I walked away from Dodd, approached the sheriff, and, in private, told him that I was convinced that Barbara Butler's murderer had struck again. The sheriff allowed that Kettering detectives had examined the marks on the schoolgirl's neck and said that they were "something like" the unusual marks they had seen on Miss Butler's neck the preceding June. "The Butler girl wasn't battered up like this girl tonight," Bradley added, "but we think that most of the Duchnowski girl's injuries are due to her body having been dragged through the woods after she was dead." I pointed Dodd out to the sheriff and told him of Dodd's desire to photograph the death scene in infrared. The sheriff had a different wish: "I'd like to talk to that guy about this case. . . . See if you can get him to come voluntarily to my office in Xenia. If he comes of his own free will, we can do our talking without having to mention Miranda."

154

I went back to Dodd and told him, "The sheriff can't let you back in the woods for your picture, but he'd like to talk to you in his office if you are willing."

"It's getting late," Dodd replied. "I better be getting home. . . . I've got to get up early and go to work in the morning."

A few minutes later the little girl's body, wrapped in a tarpaulin, was brought out of the woods and placed in an ambulance. Bradley said that plans were for the remains to be taken in the morning to Cincinnati, where Dr. Frank P. Cleveland, Hamilton County coroner and one of the most respected men in his field in the state, had agreed to perform an autopsy for Greene County Coroner Dr. J. G Krause

On the way home Dodd told me, "There's a gravel pit right near those woods that would be a nice place for a murder."

Then he advised me: "Bill, the guy who did this thing last night is the same guy who did the one last summer. . . You can make him give himself up if you want to."

"How do I do that?"

"Write a newspaper story about me. . . . You have notes and tape recordings of all the wonderful things that I sensed about these two crimes. . . You have often thought of writing me up, but you never have. . . . You have been afraid that you would get ridicule from others if you wrote about me and then I could not continue to prove myself . . . so you kept silent. . . . Therefore, I am unknown . . that is why I was not permitted to go into the woods tonight Now I tell you that you have only to inform the people of my powers, and the killer will confess himself."

I considered Dodd's proposal to be as insane as it was impossible for me to comply with

24

Events now moved swiftly toward a climax.

Greene County Coroner Dr. J. G. Krause formally ruled Regina Duchnowski's death a homicide following an autopsy performed by Dr Frank P. Cleveland at the Hamilton

County morgue in Cincinnati on the morning and early afternoon of Wednesday, December 18.

Krause, an osteopathic physician in his private practice, revealed these findings

—Cause of death is asphyxia due to strangulation.

—The discontinuous marks on the neck suggest a pattern from the clothing, and also what could be hand marks and a ligature mark on the left side of the neck . . . There are no marks on the back of the neck.

—There is no apparent or outward indication of sexual molestation. (Slide tests determined later that the killer masturbated upon the body.)

—There are multiple bruises and injuries all over the body. . . . Many of the injuries, including the injury to the back, are probably due to her having been dragged through the woods, picked up, and then thrown down by the fallen tree. . . . It cannot be stated for a certainty that any of the injuries are due to blows as there is no tearing of the [victim's] nails or other outward signs of a struggle.

—Time of death is sometime between five and nine o'clock on Monday evening.

Krause added that the victim's sweatshirt and shoes were still missing, but that her eyeglasses, which had been unaccounted for at first, were later found "in the same wooded area near the body."

About 2:30 P.M. on Wednesday I entered the detective section of the Kettering Police Department and asked Lieutenant Albert Horn, "Have you heard about the autopsy report on the Duchnowski girl?"

Horn smiled at me and replied, "No, I haven't . . . have you?"

"I heard Dr. Krause read me the findings less than an hour ago and came straight here from Cincinnati. . . . You people have been avoiding saying that there's a connection between the Butler and Duchnowski murders, but there can't be any question any more. . . . That little girl's autopsy is almost a word-for-word rewrite of Butler's!"

"Is that so?" Horn replied. "Sit down and tell me about it."

I had only had some three hours' sleep in two days but was still able to think· This guy's got to be putting me on. . . . He just can't be so calm about this . . . so unconcerned. . . . Something's happened that I don't know about.

I opened my notebook and said, "Lieutenant, you just listen to this: death by strangulation . . . discontinuous marks on the neck . . . no indication of any sexual molestation . . . no tearing of the nails or other outward signs of a struggle."

I shut the notebook, glared at the detective, and said, "Well?"

"Sounds a lot like the stuff we heard last summer, doesn't it?" Horn replied nonchalantly.

"A lot like!" I shouted. "It's the same damn thing! What's goin' on?"

"Maybe I ought to get the chief down here to hear this."

"Please do!"

Horn left the room. Several minutes passed, and then he returned, followed by Chief Shryock. The chief sat down in a chair opposite me, crossed his legs, smiled, and said, "Well, Lieutenant Horn tells me that you think these two murders were committed by the same man."

I read my notes back again, adding, "Not only that, but both victims disappeared at the same time of day and both bodies were found about twenty-five hours later. . . . That's a few too many similarities to be just a coincidence, don't you think?"

"You know the Butler case as well as I do," Shryock responded. "You have your opinions, and I have mine. I'm not saying that we disagree. But you are a newspaperman and I'm a police chief. Do you remember the Sam Sheppard case?"

"Yeah, sure."

"Then you know that police officers aren't supposed to talk to the press before the trial, don't you?"

"Oh, I get it—yesterday I was the guy you needed help from . . . but now I'm the big, bad newspaperman. Listen! That God-damned clairvoyant that you put me onto said Monday night that a girl was in pain and it would be her back—well, it was!"

"Bill, we appreciate your help," Horn said. "Maybe you'll be getting a call later on and then all that typing up of stuff that you did last summer will prove real useful."

"Okay," I said, "just as long as you get him—I've got two daughters myself, you know."

I left the police station and returned to the newspaper building. Jayne Ellison had some news for me.

"The doctors called an hour or so ago," she said. "They feel that Dodd is a colossal phony with no ESP!"

"What else did they say?" I asked.

"I'll read my notes: They think that he's very clever . . . may be compulsive . . . possibly a rare, true paranoid . . . which would be a one-in-a-thousand mental-cases type. They feel that they were able to disassociate him from reality four or five times, but he was able to snap back each time . . . he probably would crack up under pressure if it is applied gently enough . . . but under rough questioning would likely become defensive and cover up. They are of the opinion that he had entirely too much information about the Butler killing . . . the police should hear the tape and look for that garage . . . they feel that the information concerning that garage is very important . . . they also think that you contribute to what he says in that he looks to you for signals of approval . . . they are very, very sad about this young girl's murder."

"Nobody but the poor girl's family is any sorrier about that than I am," I said, and walked out the door.

I went home, had two drinks, pawed at my supper, and then, at about seven o'clock, the phone rang. It was Norman Dodd. "Were you in Cincinnati today at the autopsy?" he asked.

"Yes."

"Tell me one thing: was she sexually molested?"

"Apparently not . . . why do you ask?"

"Because if she wasn't sexually molested there is no excuse for what he did."

"What?"

"This fellow likes unmarried, clean young girls . . . preferably women. But I've got to put a stop to it now. . . . I'm going down and get him and make him turn himself in."

Dodd hung up.

I was tired and confused. I went to bed.

Three hours passed as if they were only three minutes. Someone was slapping me in the face and screaming, "Bill, Bill, wake up! They've got him!"

It was my wife, Charlotte, who was hitting me, trying to bring me back to consciousness. "What? What are you saying?" I asked.

"The killer . . . they've got him! Get up! An operator at the *News* has a message for you from the Kettering police."

I staggered out of bed, picked up the telephone, and said, "Yes?"

A woman's voice, which I knew to be that of the night switchboard operator at the newspaper, informed me: "The Kettering police phoned a few minutes ago—about ten-thirty. An apprehension has been made in the Duchnowski case and the suspect—the driver of a 1963 Pontiac, tan in color—is being arraigned now. . . . Chief Shryock will have further details at a news conference at eleven o'clock in the Kettering Municipal Court Building."

I tore off my pajamas, pulled on some clothing, and ran out the door to my car.

My apartment was on the north side of Dayton—some ten miles from Kettering. Every block of the way seemed a mile.

Chief Shryock's news conference was just beginning when I arrived. I opened the door of the crowded courtroom, stepped inside, blinked because of the many television lights, and then heard the chief say:

"The suspect is a white male, twenty years old. . . . He was arrested at seven-twenty-five this evening. . . . We had been looking for him from the beginning. . . . Detectives observed him in his car on Woodman Drive, stopped him, talked to him—and as a result of this, arrested him.

"It has been hectic," the chief continued. "We've been going hammer and tongs . . . but we have reason to believe and evidence that we have found our man. . . . The information supplied by young Tim Hart was most valuable. . . . His descriptions of the car and the driver were good and he was fairly close on the license number—one of the aspects being that he gave us a double eight instead of just one eight.

"The suspect, who has been known to us in the past, is being held without bond after being arraigned on a charge of abduction resulting in death." Shryock explained that the charge was a capital offense in Ohio. He said that the suspect "has made statements to us . . . but was duly advised of his rights before being interrogated." He claimed that "every man on the force deserves credit for the apprehension."

I looked around the room. No Dodd . . . nobody but police and newsmen. Then, just before I was about to burst with impatience, the chief identified the suspect as—Billy Joe Dean!

At that I very nearly blew my mind. The first guy, I realized, the very first suspect they had in the Butler case . . . the same guy who attacked a girl in the Ontario Store parking lot nine months before Barbara Butler's murder. . . . Dodd said something about "a year back." . . . Dodd picked up Dean's picture and studied it the night we gave him Rhine's test. . . . He said Dean didn't do it. . . . Dean got out of the Butler case because he passed a lie detector test. . . . Dodd said to pick him up again and ask him a subnormal question so he can't channel his mind—that's how he beat the test the first time.

Shryock droned on: "The suspect has been provided with a VIP attorney and has pleaded not guilty, and reserved the right to later enter a plea of not guilty by reason of insanity. This is as fine a Christmas present as I've ever had!"

I felt sick.

After the formal news conference was over I approached the chief and started to say, "This is the same guy who—"

"I know how you feel," he cut me off, "but I can't say anything—I don't want to lose this case on a technicality."

On the afternoon of Thursday, December 19, I was told by Montgomery County Prosecutor Lee C. Falke that the reason why Dean's 1967 charge of armed robbery was reduced to the probational offense of robbery was a technicality: "They screwed it up . . . violated his rights," the prosecutor claimed, "so we had to reduce the charge."

Later that afternoon I went to Billy Joe Dean's neighborhood and found there: a white wooden garage, a two-story house directly in front of it, an apartment building with aluminum-type doors to the side of it, and an alley and an apartment building with garages on the first floor to the rear of it.

Still later Jayne Ellison told me that the psychiatrists "feel certain that there is a connection between Dodd and Dean . . . you've got to connect those two!"

About 6:00 P.M. I phoned Dodd and said, "I want the truth—do you know Billy Joe Dean?"

"Why, yes," Dodd replied matter-of-factly, "I work with the fella. But he's always been the distant type . . . not my dish, so to speak. . . . He never participated when we told vulgar stories in the washroom."

"All this time . . . all these months—you knew him! Is that right?"

"Yes . . . I worked right next to him on the track . . . but the picture you folks ran of him in the paper tonight . . ."

Dodd gasped.

". . . Ah, that is . . . that picture . . . I mean he had considerably longer hair . . . I mean . . ."

"Never mind," I said. "I know God-damned well what you mean! Just tell me one more thing: *why* would anyone want to murder a twelve-year-old girl?"

"Haven't you heard about the demon?"

"The demon!"

"Yes. . . . Don't you know that many people feel that the only way they can get rid of their sins is to transfer them into an innocent body?"

"No," I sighed, "I'm afraid I don't know about those things . . . too naive, maybe . . . or too normal."

"Well, I've always appreciated reality myself. But this guy, he used to tell me about all these frustrations he had inside of him . . . the lust would build up. . . . I would try to help him . . . but he had to get the devil out. I saw it happening again—another murder—but nobody would heed what I told them. So he relinquished himself to a disciple of a demon, or to the demon himself. By the way, I would like to attend this fellow's trial. . . . I would listen with interest to the testimony the psychiatrists have to say about him. Can I count on you to help me get in the courtroom?"

"Norman, I'll try my damnedest to do that. And if nobody believes what I tell them about you, I might just put it all down in a book someday."

Epilogue

This story, as of the writing, has no ending in the sense of a pat conclusion with all the loose ends tied together in an attractive bow adorning a pretty package of justice triumphant.

On December 20, 1968, the man identified on these pages as Billy Joe Dean was committed to the Lima, Ohio, State Hospital for thirty days of psychiatric observation to determine his sanity.

On January 20, 1969, Dr. G. N. Wilson, superintendent of the Lima State Hospital, signed a statement which held, in the opinion of the hospital staff, that Dean "does not understand the nature and quality of the charges to be brought against him and cannot counsel in his own defense. He would, therefore, be considered presently insane."

Dean was, however, subsequently indicted by a Montgomery County grand jury on the charge of abduction resulting in Regina Duchnowski's death.

During a January, 1969, session of a sanity hearing to determine Dean's fitness to stand trial, Dr. Joseph Berest, a Lima staff psychiatrist, testified that the accused was insane. Berest added that the "persuading factor" in his decision was "the episode of January 4, 1969." On that date, according to the psychiatrist, Dean, "being confused and disturbed—attempted suicide by slashing his wrists with a piece of glass."

On March 20, 1969, Montgomery County Common Pleas Court Judge Cecil Edwards, who had been presiding over the sanity hearing, ruled Dean insane and committed him to an indefinite term in the Lima Hospital.

Two years passed. Then, in August of 1971, Lima Hospital officials revealed that in their opinion Dean had been "restored to reason." In October of 1971, Montgomery County Common Pleas Court Judge Stanley F. Phillips ruled Dean able to counsel in his own defense and fit to stand trial.

Dean pleaded innocent and innocent by reason of insanity

to the charge of abduction resulting in the death of the Duchnowski girl. He waived a trial by jury. His trial before a three judge panel began on February 7, 1972. On February 15, 1972, Judges Stanley F. Phillips, Fred Kramer, and Robert Tague found Dean guilty, ruled him legally sane at the time of the December 1968 crime, and sentenced him to life imprisonment.

Two days later, on February 17, 1972, Kettering Police made statements indicating that they considered the Barbara Ann Butler case solved. Montgomery County Prosecutor Lee C. Falke stated that he had evidence that Dean "was involved" in Miss Butler's death. But, he added, he did not have enough evidence to bring Dean to trial in the Butler case. Kettering Chief of Police John Shryock was quoted as saying that Dean "knew details of the Butler case that no one else would have had a way of knowing."

Dean's attorneys contended that, "If such evidence (linking Dean to the Butler murder) is or was available it should be presented to the grand jury for it's consideration. . ." Dean's attorneys also indicated that they would appeal the verdict in the Duchnowski case.

Prior to Dean's trial, Kettering police refused to comment on the record about a possible connection between the Butler and Duchnowski homicides. A detective who worked on both cases told me in private, however, that he was "personally convinced" that one person killed both girls and that both murders were committed near "the same gravel pit." This same detective also said that his opinion of the reliability of polygraph examinations had changed to the extent that "I know now that it doesn't do any good to give a nut a lie box."

Norman Dodd, to my knowledge, has never received any previously published mention of his association with these cases. Dodd phoned me a number of times in the winter and early spring of 1969. This man, who had formerly been able to perceive obscure facts merely by "sensing" them (or so he had claimed), now seemed to be seeking information by quite normal means of perception—by asking questions. He asked about the police attitude toward himself and the proceedings against Dean. My answers were as vague as I could make them. Dodd also made a number of predictions during these phone calls: "I see something dreadful happening to you crossing the street!" "I must warn you against allowing your wife to go to the store by herself—terrible things can happen to a woman in a store parking lot." "There may be another murder."

My last contact with Dodd was in a phone call he made to my home shortly before 9:00 P.M. on the evening of April 9, 1969. He began by telling me "a fourteen-year-old girl is missing" (none was as far as I could determine in a later check with police). He asked me, "Have you been thinking about haunted houses lately?" I replied that I hadn't been, but admitted that "Somebody threw a rotten egg at the front of our apartment tonight with such force that the shell is still stuck in the shingles over the door." (We had experienced a number of similar molestations in recent evenings.) He told me he "couldn't remember the name of that fellow the police got." I asked, "Do you mean Dean?" The supposed seer then responded, "Oh, that was his name, was it?" The conversation ended with Dodd saying, "Stay out of the streets yourself."

I neither know nor care what Dodd meant to imply in that parting comment. I do believe, however, that at the very least he filled in some gaps in the mystery of Barbara Butler's death that no other source, to my knowledge, has been able to fill.

I now have this picture of what happened:

The girl came out of the store pushing her cart full of purchases. As she approached her car, a man offered to assist her by lifting her packages into her car. She was then forced into her car and taken to a remote place and strangled. The ligature, perhaps, left no marks on the nape and throat because of the cushioning effects of the scarf she was wearing about her neck. The time 5:43 may very well have been important to the case—perhaps more so than the 8:00 P.M. to 2:00 A.M. approximate time of death stated by the coroner. The body was pushed down upon the floor of the Volkswagen and covered with a blanket to conceal it during the drive from the murder scene to the white garage. The car remained there until after nightfall, when it was returned to the lot in the manner Dodd described in detail.

The murder mystery, then, probably arose by chance, fed itself on the mistakes of many parties, and at length grew into an enormous enigma as the result of the maneuverings of several persons.

But what about the mystery of Norman Dodd himself?

Is he clairvoyant? In the summer and fall of 1968 Dodd demonstrated that he knew a number of facts about the

Butler case, including some obscure information. In December of 1968 Dodd told me that he knew Regina Duchnowski's accused slayer. It is easier for me to believe that Dodd obtained his information though some normal means—such as conversations with another person—than it is for me to believe that he obtained his facts from being psychic, and thus able to sense them.

If Dodd is not clairvoyant, but wished in 1968 to obtain public recognition of himself as being so, he needed the assistance of several parties in order to bring attention to himself. I assume, from what he told me in December of 1968, that his desired means to this end was a newspaper story documenting his abilities. He was aware of obscure facts in the Butler case. But how could he make others aware of his knowledge? Would a genuine, publicity-shy clairvoyant approach a newspaperman and begin demonstrating his psychic powers? From what Dr. Rhine told me, a genuine clairvoyant would not do this—and neither did Dodd. I approached him after being told about him by a woman who had written a letter to the police suggesting the use of a clairvoyant. I was quite impressed by the things Dodd told me about the murder case. But his knowledge was not limited to the murder—he also knew obscure facts about me, my family, and Dr. Rhine.

If Dodd is not clairvoyant, how did he know about the picture in my wallet, my wife's concern about her second pregnancy, the fact that my wife had been shopping for red shoes, and the happenings in our apartment in December of 1968? My wife and I asked ourselves this same question. We answered it by realizing that our professed friend, Linda Keagan, knew about the picture in my wallet, had listened to my wife say she was concerned about the possibility of twins in her second pregnancy, had taken my wife shopping on the day that she tried on the reddish-orange shoes, and was in our apartment on the afternoon in December when things were done and matters discussed that Dodd was able to "sense" that evening.

When Dodd was "hitting" me with these things—and as a result making me feel almost certain at times that he was clairvoyant—I never suspected that he and Linda were in any way acquainted. She was my wife's friend.

But in the clearer light of reflection the above seemed to us to be a few too many items of knowledge common to Dodd and Linda Keagan to be pure coincidence. And there

166

was more: Linda had told us that she knew of the allegedly pregnant girl at the newspaper and had expressed animosity toward her. . . . Linda was one of the persons we told about our purchase of a gun—after which the door knockings abruptly ceased. When we added the fact that it was Linda who had told me about Drake's weak stomach just prior to Dodd's telling me about a suspect with a weak stomach, we became convinced that Linda and Norman Dodd had done a considerable amount of talking to one another.

In March of 1969 I asked Dr. Rhine if he had any explanation for Dodd's knowledge of his ailments. Rhine's answer: "Well, the fakers are organized . . . therefore it wouldn't surprise me in the least if these people who are trying to prove themselves clairvoyant for profit would get together to exchange information." Rhine, however, said he could not rule out the possibility that Dodd had some "irregular and completely undisciplined" form of ESP—"the value of his ability being highly doubtful."

There remain, I must admit, some open ends—some portion of Dodd's "sensings" for which I have no logical explanation other than to class them as educated guesses (e.g., Dodd's knowledge, in December of 1968, that the stock market was going to drop . . . his knowledge of the policeman outside the *Daily News* building . . . and his sensing, in a newspaper elevator, that the managing editor was about to receive an important phone call).

Why would a person who is not clairvoyant go to great lengths in an attempt to gain recognition of himself as being clairvoyant? I recall Dodd's own words: "Some of those charlatans make a million dollars a year off the suckers." There is nothing unusual about a man's working and scheming for a lifetime if he believes the end result of his labors will be a million dollars. The motivation behind Dodd's wish to be accepted as clairvoyant is, then, less of a mystery to me than is the answer to this question: Why was such a clever and ambitious person unable to make his way in life in some more lucrative or prestigious way than that of a factory worker? As for his collaborators in this affair—as I have said, a person who is not clairvoyant could not even have gotten his plan off the ground without help— only those persons themselves know why they did what logic tells me they must have done.

Dodd is, apparently, not finished with his association with mysteries. He created one of his own sometime prior to the fall of 1970 by moving from his home without leaving a forwarding address.

My family and I have also been wanderers in the wake of the murders. In the spring of 1969 I accepted the probability that the mystery of the girl on the Volkswagen floor would never be solved officially. I also realized that I could not do justice to both my newspaper job and a writing of this account. My wife insisted that the latter task was the one of prime importance—even though it would mean the uprooting of our children from their native surroundings and a financial sacrifice from which we might never recover.

In May of 1969 I resigned from my job and moved my family from Dayton. In our case the price of involvement was very high. My wife tells me that it has cost me my sense of humor. I know that it has made me a cautious and suspicious person. I will always be disturbed by the tragedy of the Duchnowski girl's death because I believe I was, in a way, given early warning of it. I alerted other people, but they would not believe me until they found the body. Perhaps a reading of this story will someday condition someone to believe what he does not wish to believe and cause him to get involved in time to save a life. If that happens just once, then I will know that the reward of my involvement exceeded the price.